LITERACY ASSESSMENT IN PRACTICE

LANGUAGE ARTS

Education Department of South Australia

ACKNOWLEDGEMENTS

Developed by the Assessment of Writing and Reading Inservice Teacher Education (AWRITE) project team:
Lynne Badger, Mike Dilena, Judy Peters, Colleen Webster and Betty Weeks

With the assistance of the following classroom teachers:

Pia Adams
Barbara Agnew
Kingsley Allen
Kaye Bryant
Sue Caddy
Cherie Cleary
Julie Dawson
Debbie Greenslade
Peggy Hirsch
Penny Maxwell
Ann McLoughlin
Cheryl Nankivell

Meredith Nankivell
Sharon Pash
Cheryl Rafferty
Andrew Ray
Dzintra Richards
Kevin Siemonek
Leanne Taylor
Bronwyn Ward
Bob Wildy
Paula Willson
Debbie Wyatt
Anna Young

Typing and layout: Rachel Grossmann

Distributed in the United States by: The National Council of Teachers of English, 1111 W. Kenyon Road, Urbana, Illinois 61801-1096

Cataloguing-in-publication :

428	Literacy assessment in practice : R-7 language arts. -
LIT	[Adelaide] : Education Department of S. Aust., 1991.
DDC 20 :	137p. : ill.
428.007	1. Literacy - study and teaching

ISBN 0 7243 8151 1
ASCIS order no. : 670274

© Education Department of South Australia, 1991
Produced by the Darlington Materials Development Centre
Printed by A. J. Secker, Director and Government Printer, South Australia
ISBN 0 7243 8151 1
W1649

FOREWORD

Over the last two decades literacy teaching has changed dramatically. New understandings about language and literacy learning have challenged many traditional practices. At the same time, fundamental changes to Australia's population, family structures and social mores have caused schools to adapt teaching to different sets of needs. Now, more than ever before, schools are preparing students for a diverse, technically complex world which demands ever increasing standards of literacy.

As a consequence the Education Department of South Australia has given particular attention to the teaching of language arts, guiding teachers by means of language arts curriculum documents and inservice programs such as the Early Literacy Inservice Course (ELIC) and the Literacy and Learning in the Middle Years (LLIMY) project. These literacy teaching programs are making available to all primary schools the expertise that teachers have developed as they have confronted new challenges.

New approaches to teaching, however, require assessment methods that reflect the achievements that students make as they undertake new and demanding literacy tasks. Assessment methods that reflect only a narrow part of what students learn are no longer adequate and schools have recognised the need for sensible and practical ways of monitoring students' progress.

This need was reflected in the report of the Primary Review conducted by the Education Department of South Australia (1988). The Review revealed an uncertainty among many teachers about ways of assessing students' achievements in literacy. In 1988 the AWRITE (Assessment in Writing and Reading Inservice Teacher Education) project was set up to begin to address this uncertainty. Twenty four primary teachers, one from each of the State's school districts, were chosen to work for six months with three key teachers from the LLIMY project and two consultants from the South Australian College of Advanced Education.

Over the six months of the project the participating teachers explored a range of possible assessment approaches in their classrooms. The outcome is a wealth of practical knowledge, much of which has been gathered together in this resource book.

Ken Boston
Director General of Education

CONTENTS

1 LITERACY ASSESSMENT : THE CHALLENGES

Teachers confront a number of critical challenges in assessing children's literacy in ways that reflect current insights into literacy development and are inclusive of all groups of students in our classrooms. Among these challenges are:

1.   Assessment that is comprehensive and balanced

You need to know *what* to look for. You want information that is comprehensive, that gives you a full picture of growing readers and writers. At the same time you do not want to be overwhelmed by too much detail. You want to know what is important in all this information.

2.   Assessment for teaching

You need to know what assessment techniques are available to you, and the extent to which the information they provide will help you assess your students' achievements and needs. The major purpose for assessment is to provide you with information that will help you better understand and meet your students' needs.

3.   Assessment for students

Your students are more likely to succeed if they know what is expected of them, what they have achieved and what is needed for further achievement. Therefore, your assessment methods will need to provide information to students so they can monitor their own progress and move towards successful independent learning. Assessment will thus provide a means to help students to help themselves.

4. Assessment for parents and caregivers

Few parents and caregivers have experienced the intense literacy learning that now takes place in most primary classrooms. They want to know what their children are doing and what are the things that you see as indications of progress. They want evidence of what their children have achieved and they want to know what kinds of things their children find difficult. If you can provide them with detailed information about their children and seek further information from them, you and they can become partners in these students' progress.

5. Assessment that is practical

If gathering and recording information about your students has to be done in addition to the normal load of teaching, you will be overwhelmed and probably teach less effectively. So you will need assessment methods that become part of normal classroom activities.

6. Assessment that is systematic

Deciding what you want to assess, how to do it and how to communicate to students, parents and caregivers is only one part of having a systematic approach to assessment. The other crucial part of this process is your plan for when you will make time for information to be collected, how often it will be done, by whom and how it will be stored.

This resource book sets out to meet these six challenges. It deals with:
- how to develop a systematic approach to assessment
- what information you might gather
- how you and your students might gather this information
- the constraints of various techniques of assessment
- ways in which you and your students might document the information you gather
- how you might communicate with parents and caregivers.

Implicit in the above is a view of students as active learners, interested in their own progress and willing to take increasing responsibility for their own learning.

In developing your assessment program it is important to note that assessment practices need to address the special learning needs of all groups of students, particularly girls, Aboriginal students, students from non-English speaking backgrounds, students in poverty, students with disabilities and students in isolated settings.

By working with your students to experiment with and adapt the various ideas and strategies in this book you are likely to develop more mutually rewarding teacher-student relationships. You will also be more aware of the ways in which your assessment practices signal to students, parents and caregivers what is important and valued in the curriculum.

2 USING THIS BOOK TO PLAN YOUR ASSESSMENT PRACTICES

If your approach to assessment is going to be an effective and manageable means of fostering students' learning and helping you to evaluate your literacy program then you need to plan your practices in a systematic and decisive way. The purpose of this chapter is to suggest a process for using this book to plan a comprehensive and effective assessment system in your classroom. The important feature of the six step process described below is that it puts you firmly in control of the book and helps you make decisions that relate specifically to your needs and those of your students.

This kind of control is necessary because this resource book offers more options than you could possibly take up. You need to be selective. As you confront the issues raised in this book you will be making your own decisions about what you want to do. These decisions will be guided by the particular literacy program you offer and your own perceptions of your students' needs as readers and writers. No-one else can make these decisions for you because assessment must be tied to what you teach. They are not separate issues but must be planned together.

The chapters of this book provide a great deal of information on which to base your decisions about what to assess, how to assess, how to store information and how to communicate to students, parents, caregivers and others. Therefore, like any resource book, this one is meant to be dipped into and used by you according to your own questions or needs. It is not a prescription or a set of recipes. What it does provide is a comprehensive framework for defining and organising all the various aspects of literacy which might need to be considered in literacy assessment. There is also a range of practical ideas which you can use, adapt and modify.

SIX MANAGEABLE STEPS
You can systematically plan your assessment practices by breaking down the decisions you have to make into six manageable steps.

Step 1: Clarify what you need to assess

Clarify exactly what it is about your students' reading and writing that you need to assess. Chapter 3 contains a framework for assessment of reading and writing with the acronym CAASR. If you want to foster students' literacy development you need to collect data about each aspect of this framework. So the first step is to review your present assessment practices, to help you identify clearly what you currently assess. You can then make decisions about what other information you will need to include so that you cover each of the categories of CAASR.

Step 2: Decide how you will collect the information you need

Once you have established what to assess and therefore what information you require, you then have to decide how you will collect this information. You can examine your current techniques and compare them with the six described in Chapter 4 to decide if you need to add any of these to your repertoire. Next you can decide how you want to store the information you have documented (see Chapter 5).

Step 3: Record your decisions

Most of the AWRITE teachers found it useful to draw up some sort of overview chart to record their decisions about how they would assess students' progress in each area of the CAASR framework. Appendix 2 shows one teacher's assessment overview chart. In addition to recording planning decisions he includes a column on "Program Implications/Action". In this section he includes all the things he will need to teach and organise to ensure that his system works.

In planning your own system you will need to make decisions about these things. Chapter 6, "Communicating information", gives some ideas about what you have to think about here. Many of the organisational details you need to consider can also be found in Chapter 4 under the "Organising" sub-heading for each information collecting technique.

Step 4: Draw up an assessment calendar

While your decisions about what to assess and how to do it constitute a major part of developing any assessment plan you need then to organise more specifically the practical aspects of when you will do it and how often information will be collected. One way to deal with this is to draw up a rough calendar for the year and mark in the times when you have to communicate to parents about students' progress. An example of one teacher's calendar is shown on the next page.

	Term 1	Term 2	Term 3	Term 4
1				
2				
3	Parent info. night	Newsletter to parents	Newsletter to parents	Newsletter to parents
4				
5				
6	Newsletter to parents			
7				
8	Parent interviews	Written reports		Written reports
9		Inteview as requested		
10			Interview as requested	

Although reporting on students' progress is only one purpose for assessing, it does provide a set of key times during the year when you have to summarise the information you have about students. It therefore provides a focus for organising your assessment plan. How you organise your own calendar depends on factors such as your own preferences and the school policy on assessment and communicating with parents and caregivers.

Step 5: Plan a more detailed assessment timeline
Once you have identified your focus times for assessment it is necessary to think clearly about how, on a week to week basis, you can ensure that you do in fact gather the information you need. There are no hard and fast rules about the frequency with which you need to collect information about students on either an individual or group basis. This again will depend on what you are teaching and what you therefore need to know about students' development at any particular time. There are times though when your focus on collecting information may be more intense. The most obvious of these is the first term with a new class when you need to find out as much as possible, as quickly as possible, to help you to know what the students can do and to plan appropriate experiences to build on their strengths.

Other times for this more intense focus may be when you:
• want to monitor a new aspect of your literacy program
• want to make a decision about changes to classroom reading resources
• need to report to parents on students' progress
• want to make changes to aspects of your literacy program
• want to investigate a particular student's development

One of the problems you, like other teachers, may have experienced is the almost overwhelming difficulty of consistently collecting information on all the students in your class. As is indicated in

Chapter 4 of this book, you can organise your data collecting so that the students themselves are responsible for certain aspects of it. You will need to decide exactly which information the students can be responsible for and how they will go about doing it. The section in Chapter 4 on "Drawing on student record-keeping and self-assessment", pp.66-76, provides some useful ideas and starting points for you to consider.

The example in Appendix 3 shows one junior primary teacher's tentative assessment "diary" for a year. Naturally this plan would be subject to change during the course of the year as the need arises.

Step 6: Plan a weekly timetable

While calendars and diaries of the kind described above give a detailed overview of when information is collected, one further step will help to ensure that, given the many pressures which act on you every day in the classroom, the information you need is actually collected.

This involves you in specifically 'ear-marking' times in your weekly timetable for collecting assessment information. One way of doing this is by drawing up a weekly timetable such as the one in Appendix 4 to plan exactly when you will collect information during the course of any particular day. In this example, not all the information gathering times are obvious because they occur as part of the teaching sessions, e.g. observing student reading and writing in a science project, or during social education activities.

These six steps are only one way to approach the process of planning a comprehensive and effective assessment system in your classroom. You may devise a different planning process. If you work with other teachers who are interested in further developing their own classroom assessment practices you can gain the kind of support which helps you to take on and successfully confront the challenges posed by this book. However, no matter what process you use, the outcome must be a plan that you can use to successfully monitor your students' progress and to foster their literacy learning.

3   CAASR : A FRAMEWORK FOR LITERACY ASSESSMENT

Assessment involves gathering information about students and using this information to make decisions about the students' progress and development. This information is also used to help you evaluate your program. Inevitably the particular information you choose to gather has a profound effect on what happens in your classroom. The aspects that you focus on assume enormous status. These are the things that students and parents see as important. These are the things you are seen to value. These are the things that students think are worth working for.

Unavoidably, then, assessment shapes the curriculum. For this reason, assessment needs to focus on just those things that you want your teaching to achieve. To do this it is useful to have a framework for assessment that is both comprehensive and balanced in terms of:
• what is known about good literacy teaching
• what aspects of literacy are appropriate for the particular group of students you teach.

This chapter presents a framework for assessing reading and writing which draws on information about good literacy teaching. It thus suggests certain key aspects that need to be considered. Without them your assessment may be seen as either narrow or unbalanced. At the same time the framework provides adequate scope for the particular teaching that is appropriate to the students you teach. Lying behind the framework presented is the view that some aspects of assessment and teaching need to be included by every teacher, but the details or emphasis are determined by the needs of your particular students and the decisions you make to help this development.

The framework presented is called CAASR. The letters of this acronym stand for the five different kinds of information that will help you assess your students':
• Concepts about literacy
• Attitudes to writing and reading
• Aspects of written products and comprehension
• Strategies for writing and reading
• Range of writing and reading

The CAASR framework reflects the understandings about literacy which teachers have been developing over the last two decades. As such it is offered as a distillation of what teachers and researchers currently know and as a signpost to what we need to develop. As reading and writing are so closely related, the same acronym is applicable to both.

In the sections which follow Concepts about literacy are described first, because they apply to both reading and writing. Attitudes to writing, Aspects of written products and Strategies for writing are next described in that order. The specific reading elements of the framework then follow: Attitudes to reading, Aspects of comprehension and Strategies for reading. Finally, you'll find a section on the Range of reading and writing which students need to experience.

Overviews of the frameworks for writing and reading can be found at the end of this chapter (pp.37-38). You might like to read these first so you know what to expect. They give you a quick reference to all the parts of CAASR for easy access when planning and programming. A simpler version can be found in Appendix 1.

CAASR : CONCEPTS ABOUT LITERACY
When students come to school it is reasonable to expect that each has had some experience of literacy. However, the concepts students have about what literacy is used for and how it works depend upon the particular kinds of experiences they have had in the home, the school and the wider community.

The students' understanding of what literacy is used for, and the satisfactions it gives, provides a powerful and sustaining impetus for them to learn how to use literacy in these ways for themselves. To understand and track students' literacy development then it is necessary to know about students' awareness of these concepts, and how they expand them over the year.

Documenting and recording information about these concepts has the potential to develop better understandings about why students are developing as they are or, as may be the case, why they are not developing. An analysis of the students' behaviours and the programs provided for them may reveal that they are experiencing difficulties because it is assumed that they have had experiences which they have not in fact had. In this case students' difficulties may then be seen more as a lack of experience than as a defect in the student. The obvious implication here is that teachers need to find out what experiences students have had and then plan ways of building on them through classroom literacy programs.

From the point of view of assessment tasks, what are the concepts that can be monitored? At this stage the following categories of concepts are offered:

- Uses for written language
- Kinds of written products
- The possible range of audiences
- The appropriate use of written language
- The similarities and differences between speech and writing
- The processes readers and writers use.

Uses for written language

Students' understandings of what written language can be used for are critical to their development as readers, writers and as members of society. Students are more likely to act powerfully in the world if they can use language for a variety of purposes. Students from non-English speaking backgrounds (NESB) may have understandings of written language uses for both their home language and for English.

The following is the range of written language uses which are consistently listed in literature on language arts:
- to record (feelings, observations, etc)
- to describe
- to inform or advise
- to persuade
- to clarify thinking
- to explore and maintain relationships
- to predict or hypothesise
- to make comparisons
- to command or direct or instruct
- to amuse or entertain.

Teachers need to monitor students' awareness of this range of purposes.

Kinds of written products

Through their experiences with a variety of texts (in English or their home language) students can come to understand the many different kinds of written products that we can make.

In the home, school and community many kinds of written products are potentially available, for example:

cards	welcomes
lists	information
memos	bills
diagrams	magazines
signs:	rules
directions	invitations
warnings	messages

charts	how to make
timetables	how to fix, etc
programs	jokes, riddles
advertisements	newsletters
pamphlets	instructions
brochures	record, tape and C.D. covers
newspapers	scoreboards
labels	T.V. and radio guides
forms	street directories
games	phone books
letters:	address books
personal	calendars
applications	picture books/short stories
information	plays
requests	fiction texts:
encyclopedias	mystery
dictionaries	historical
thesauruses	science fiction
atlases	fantasy
year books	myths/legends/folk tales
reports	adventure
cookbooks	family stories
packaging	adolescent problems
informational texts:	animal stories
history	poetry:
geography	epic poems
science	odes
medicine, etc	haiku
autobiographies	ballads
instructional manuals:	sonnets
how to do	hymns and prayers

Teachers need to monitor students' development to find out :
- which particular kinds of products they know about
- which they prefer to read and in which language
- what they know about the different kinds of products, (such as different structural and language properties)
- what they understand about the more literary dimensions of products, such as allegory and satire

The possible range of audiences
Teachers need to find out what range of readers the students know about and write for as this will influence what they write, how they write, the language they use and the kinds of feedback they may receive. NESB students may need to write in their home language for a range of these audiences.

The following are the kinds of readers students can write for:
- peers – known and unknown
- parents
- relations – cousins, uncles, aunties, grandparents
- teachers – class, other teachers in the school, teachers in other schools
- members of the community – known and unknown.

The appropriate use of written language

An essential part of learning written language is learning how to use it appropriately. Different kinds of products are written depending on what it is for and who is to read it. For instance, letters are one kind of product but writers do different things when writing a personal chatty letter to a friend from when they write to an unknown person to request information or goods.

The features of the product which vary according to purpose and audience are:
- what is written about
- the way language is used
- the style or tone
- conventions for layout and punctuation
- the kind of greeting and ending used
- the language used (English or home language).

Teachers need to monitor students' awareness of:
- variations in product according to purpose and readers
- specific kinds of variations to content, vocabulary , syntax, tone, layout, which are appropriate to different kinds of products intended for particular purposes and readers
- appropriateness of using English or their home language.

The similarities and differences between speech and writing

In order to develop as users of written language students must come to some basic understandings about the similarities and differences between oral and written modes.

Teachers need to discover whether students are aware that:
- speech and writing are different sides of the same coin – *What we can say can be written down.*
- both can be used for a variety of purposes
- both change in predictable ways according to setting, purpose and audience
- both can be used to create and explore real and imaginary worlds
- writing can be used to do different things from speech. It can, for

example, provide a permanent record which persists across time and distance and thus enables writers to review and revise ideas
- writing must use a range of devices to compensate for the lack of aspects available when we speak face to face e.g. tone, emphasis, gestures, shared context
- speech and writing differ in the way they use vocabulary and syntax and in their grammatical complexity in the settings in which they are used.

The processes readers and writers use

Learning to read and write means developing appropriate ways of operating on and with written language across a range of tasks, texts and settings. As readers and writers develop sets of competencies for using written language they also need to develop their awareness of how they go about literacy tasks.

Teachers need to find out about students':
- awareness of how they read and write
- awareness of the coping strategies which can be used to deal successfully with difficult reading and writing tasks
- actual use of these coping strategies across the curriculum
- ways of making choices about how they tackle reading and writing tasks.

CAASR : ATTITUDES TO WRITING

The energy source which fuels the act of writing is the writer's engagement with the task. Influences which affect this engagement are the writer's:
- self-concept with regard to writing
- commitment to investing time and energy in the task.

Teachers need to know about these so they can provide classroom contexts and climates which nurture young writers and provide them with the support and encouragement they need.

Self-concept

To find out how students feel about themselves as writers, and how different tasks, purposes, and forms of writing affect these feelings, teachers need to find ways of monitoring and recording:
- the circumstances in which students anticipate writing with a sense of pleasure, achievement and satisfaction
- their use of writing as a means of organising, influencing or making sense of their world
- the extent to which they use writing for their own purposes.

Commitment

Teachers also want to know about students' willingness to:

- take risks, such as using temporary spellings, and trying unusual language, or unfamiliar forms of writing
- assume responsibility for such tasks as setting and meeting deadlines, self-correcting, setting challenges, making decisions
- make changes by exploring alternative beginnings or endings
- ask for help and feedback and accept challenges
- accept uncertainty, suspend judgement, use approximations and keep issues like mechanics on hold while grappling with the larger concerns of ideas and information
- ignore distractions and stay on task, when working alone or with others
- share their writing with others, discuss insights, accept advice and give suggestions to others
- be critically reflective and use their past experiences to shape future writing.

Influences on students' self esteem and commitment

Teachers also need to find out about the possible range of influences on students' self esteem and commitment, such as:

- expectations based on gender and racial stereotyping
- poverty
- recency of migration
- recency of learning English
- history of success in learning
- attitudes to disability
- sexual, racial and other forms of harassment
- acknowledgement and valuing of students' experiences, culture and language.

CAASR : ASPECTS OF WRITTEN PRODUCTS

When analysing pieces of writing teachers are faced with an enormous range of things that they could respond to as indicators of achievement and/or progress in writing. The following four categories have been provided as a way of organising and focusing any analysis of writing:

- ideas
- organisation
- language
- mechanics.

This scheme provides a comprehensive and balanced framework within which teachers can detail all the specific things they might pay attention to in trying to document achievement in students' writing. However, in many classrooms there will be students who are literate in, or are developing literacy in languages other than English. Teachers will therefore need to be aware that students may well be able to achieve some things, when writing in their home language, that they may not be able to achieve in English. NESB students' writing may be analysed to find evidence of their use of the conventions of their home language.

13

Ideas and information

Writing is an act of thinking and every finished piece of writing is a record of thinking achievements that have been made. When students are able to engage seriously with ideas and issues which concern them the following kinds of achievements can be observed:
- topic knowledge
- knowledge of the world
- presentation of ideas.

Students' achievements can, therefore, be the focus of the teacher's attention in these areas.

Topic knowledge

Teachers can look for evidence of what students know about particular topics. Teachers can analyse students' writing to discover:
- the amount of information provided about the topic
- the depth of information
- the accuracy of the information
- the different kinds of information provided
- how the student relates ideas from different sources such as their experiences, reading or television.

Knowledge of the world

Through their experiences students develop their knowledge about the world and how it works. Teachers can look for evidence of students' understandings of:
- themselves
- others (for instance of parents as people with their own needs rather than as simply servants to children's needs)
- the relationships between people
- the complex community beyond the home
- the complex natural environment.

As well as these, teachers can also look for evidence of students' sensitivity to issues such as the stereotyping of characters or ideas, in relation to gender, race, ethnicity, disability.

Presentation of ideas

Writing provides students with the opportunity to extend and elaborate ideas – to find gaps and contradictions. They are confronted with the problem of working through ideas till they can support and justify them. Teachers can then look for evidence of:
- commitment to rationality: being prepared to support rather than simply assert generalisations
- explanation and elaboration: providing specifics, giving examples, providing evidence
- presentation and evaluation of different perspectives
- presenting own opinion or point of view
- dealing with difficult questions.

Organisation

When students write for readers they face a number of, sometimes, competing organisational demands. They may have to:
- organise their ideas and information in ways that make sense to themselves, that is they have to structure their own complex experience
- recognise the expectations generated by the particular form or genre they choose
- present what they have to say in ways that help their readers to understand/appreciate/respond/agree.

For writing to succeed six things need to be clear:
- what kind of writing it is
- what the focus is
- what the parts are
- how the parts are sequenced
- what the links between parts are
- what has been done to meet readers' needs.

When looking at students' writing teachers can focus on these six aspects.

Kinds of writing

As students explore a variety of different forms they begin to understand the ways in which different kinds of writing are organised. They gradually learn to use the organisational structures typically used (in Western European cultures) for stories and other entertainments, events, descriptions or entities (people, places, things), accounts of processes, arguments, etc. Teachers may comment to students on the way they use:
- typical story features such as:
  setting (when, who, where)
  problem or initiating event
  episodes or events developing from this
  resolution or outcome
  conclusion.

- typical patterns for describing entities and processes and for reporting events:
  statement of focus, scope and significance
  sections which explain or amplify
  concluding summary.

- patterns for simple arguments:
  what I think
  why I think this
  what others who disagree think
  why I think they are wrong
  concluding statement.

Focus	Readers respond to writing in which they can find a clear focus. Therefore, teachers may comment on the way students use:

Focus

Readers respond to writing in which they can find a clear focus. Therefore, teachers may comment on the way students use:
- titles which clearly indicate what the piece is about or which show the tone or mood
- sub-headings which clearly show that each section is part of the whole and is all about one particular sub-topic
- introductions that give direction to the whole piece
- topic sentences that give direction to sub-sections or paragraphs
- endings that summarise or clinch
- sentences that keep the focus on the topic of the previous sentence.

Parts

Readers should be able to skim and see how the parts of a piece relate to the overall focus or theme. Teachers may attend, therefore, to the way students identify parts by using:
- sub-headings
- topic sentences and key words
- paragraph indentations and spacing.

Sequences

Readers expect parts that flow one from the other in a manner appropriate to the genre and to the language in which it is written. What is seen as a typical sequence in English is not necessarily applicable to stories in other languages. For instance repetition is an important ingredient in Aboriginal stories, whereas Asian stories may have a more circular structure. When commenting, therefore, on how appropriately parts are sequenced teachers can consider:
- conformity to typical story sequence according to the language in which it is written
- whole parts - whole sequence of non narrative writing
- discourse conventions that signal direction such as first, then, next, on the one hand, on the other hand, moreover, furthermore, however, nevertheless, finally.

Links

Readers expect coherence (the whole piece being about one main topic or theme) and cohesion (all the parts clearly linking). Teachers can, therefore, analyse students' writing in terms of the following:
- topic sentences that structure a paragraph so firmly that the following sentences do not require explicit linking devices. Consider the following example:
  There are three reasons why parents are confused about their children's achievements. Traditional standardised test scores don't tell parents what their children can do, only how they compare as test values with other students. Traditional report cards don't tell parents all the wonderful things their children can do but simply provide a mark or grade which suggests a relation to some undefined "standard." Traditional means of teacher-parent communication (e.g. visiting nights) leave little time for teachers and students to tell parents all the challenges they have taken on and all the things they have achieved.

- repetition of key words that show the focus is being maintained:, e.g. "traditional," "parents," "children," in the preceding piece
- use of pronouns (he, she, it, we, they, him, her, them, us); possessive adjectives (my, your, his, her, their, our) as well as words to show focus without repeating the noun (this, that, these, those)
- elaboration of a metaphor, simile or other figure of speech over sentences or paragraphs.

Readers' needs

Writers gradually learn to shape their writing to meet readers' needs for clarity, focus, voice, vitality and interest, and form. Teachers can watch for use of:
- effective "leads" that gain and hold the readers' attention
- clear indications of what the piece is about and where it is going
- recognition of what the reader might already know and believe
- strong links that make the overall structure clear
- use of layout and graphic devices to make for easy reading
- direct address to the reader
- a conclusion or summary that brings the piece to an effective close.

Language
At times close attention needs to be given to the expression that students use in their writing. For this purpose teachers need a set of sub-categories that outlines the features of language to be focused on. A three-fold scheme of vocabulary, sentences and style is suggested.

Vocabulary

Students' use of words changes as they experience different varieties of oral discourse and as they immerse themselves in the rich and varied language of different kinds of writing. At various stages teachers may comment on such things as the use of:
- new words (as students use an increasing range of words)
- precise words
- effective adjectives, adverbs and verbs
- words that surprise and delight because of their freshness and unexpectedness
- words that make comparisons (metaphors, similes)
- words such as abstract nouns that convey the message economically,
  e.g. "His boss was delighted with his punctuality and promptness." Instead of "His boss was delighted that he was always on time and that he got things done quickly".
- words from reading that seem particularly appropriate to writing because they have an exactness, and appropriateness often lacking in speech
- words from speech that give writing vitality and vigor
- non-sexist language
- words from other languages for which English has no equivalent.

Sentences

It is important to note that all students, even those who have enjoyed the experience of being read to at home, encounter new forms of language in their school years. With rich experiences in reading and writing students' use of sentences develops in a number of directions. Teachers can respond to students' achievements by commenting on such things as their use of:

- complete grammatical sentences
- compound sentences (two simple sentences linked by "and," "but" or "or")
- complex sentences (combining a simple main clause such as "He stopped" with a subordinate such as "when he was tired")
- an appropriate balance of simple and complex sentences
- adventurous sentences which relate ideas and information in complex ways (first attempts may involve incomplete grammatical structures)
- varied sentence beginnings such as:
  a phrase before the subject:
  "At dawn, they scrambled out of their sleeping bags"
  "At the first blush of light in the east, they ..."
  a clause before the subject:
  "While the sky was just beginning to grow pink, they ..."
- sentences that use lists of words, phrases and clauses such as:
  words – "He was dirty, dishevelled and dead-tired." (Lists can comprise nouns, adjectives, verbs, adverbs)
  phrases – "She crept across the garden, through the little wood and over the wall."
  clauses – "They clambered over the steep hill, slithered down the grassy slope and trudged through the swampy valley."
- sentences with surprises such as:
  "The peace of the evening was rent into a thousand fragments."
  "He can't even make toast. Feel that. It's like coconut matting."
- sentences that pick up and develop the language (and ideas) of previous sentences
- sentences that make use of sound combinations such as the earlier example where the "d" sound is repeated in "dirty, dishevelled and dead-tired"
- sentences that build up atmosphere or particular effects.

Style

Effective pieces of writing are more than a collection of appropriate words and good sentences. They are wholes that have a consistency of tone or voice. The tones or styles that students might adopt are endless and part of the fun and challenge for students is taking on different styles and attempting different kinds of writing. Teachers can respond to these attempts by commenting on such achievements as:

- appropriateness of tone or style
- consistency of tone or style

- the building up of atmosphere
- attempts at new kinds of writing (e.g. dialogue)
- attempts at new styles or voices (e.g. writing tentatively or authoritatively)
- cohesion (through words that link with words and ideas in previous sentences).

Mechanics

Because teachers are concerned with students' growing mastery of the graphic conventions of writing they naturally look to find evidence of students' achievements in such things as handwriting, spelling, punctuation, layout. If computers or word processors are used, mastery of these tools can also be noted. So teachers look for evidence of students taking on new challenges, showing progress, and achieving mastery in the following sub-categories of mechanics.

Handwriting

Depending on the age and experience of the writer there are many aspects of achievement to be observed. For example, one focus might be on the students' development in:
- forming letters:
  "Mary is good at forming "y's" that have hooks below the line."
  "Bruno is writing most of his letters on the line."
- using spaces between words.

It is important to remember that handwriting is influenced by the students' home language so that NESB students may have different understandings about conventions such as direction. Handwriting can also be influenced by physical difficulty, by what has been learned in other countries or other states, or by instruction at home.

If handwriting is an important part of the writing curriculum – as it is with young writers – teachers can include any of the aspects of handwriting that they normally focus on. (For more specific information see *Handwriting : South Australian Modern Cursive : R-7 Language Arts*, Education Department of South Australia, 1984.)

Spelling

As with handwriting, there are many aspects of spelling that can be taken into account. The focus again will depend on the age and experience of the student. It may also depend on the ease with which certain students remember visual patterns. It will certainly depend on students' experience with literacy. There are many things teachers can focus on:
- the words the student can spell automatically:
  "Maria has shown she can spell 'said', 'was' and 'like'."
  "Rebecca spells correctly all the words on our list of the 50 words most frequently occurring in print."
- the range of words the student is attempting:

"Pia is trying difficult words such as 'enormous' and getting everything right except the 'ou' in the final syllable."
"Carl tried 'machine' and got 'mashin'."
- specific parts of words such as difficult endings (ent/ant), doubling consonants, etc.
- success in representing each of the syllables in multisyllabic words; e.g. 'beautiful'
- success in remembering the correct spelling of words previously used incorrectly in writing
- proof reading
- use of various sources to check temporary spellings.

(For more information see *Spelling : R-7 Language Arts*, Education Department of South Australia, 1984.)

Punctuation

Punctuation appropriate to various kinds of writing develops with students' experience in reading and writing. What aspects to focus on will depend on the students' stage of development. At various stages teachers may be concerned with:
- use of stops and capitals to signal sentences
- use of speech marks
- use of commas, apostrophes and exclamation marks.

Layout

Teachers, and students too, often respond to written material in terms of its physical appearance. Therefore responses can be made to issues such as:
- balance of text and illustration
- setting out in sections, pages, etc.
- use of particular graphic forms e.g. **BAM!** to create interest.

Using word processors

Computer or word processing skills which can be organised under the mechanics category include:
- setting up the machine
- loading the program
- finding the appropriate letters, spaces, capitals, etc.
- using the editing sources - deletions, corrections, insertions, etc.
- manipulating the print on the screen
- printing, saving, re-loading.

Teachers wishing to update their knowledge of current language conventions can refer to *Style Manual*, Australian Government Publishing Service, 1988.

CAASR : STRATEGIES FOR WRITING
Teachers need to know about the strategies students use because so much of students' success as writers depends on their use of an appropriate range of strategies for managing the complex process of composing a text. Through experience many of these strategies

become almost automatic in the act of writing, but when students are learning to write teachers need to make sure students know about, and experiment with, as many of them as possible.

The expanded view of the writing process which follows enables teachers to set up students for success by defining what is important at any particular point, and assessing whether or not the writer needs help. In order to describe this range the writing task has been divided into three distinct but overlapping phases:
- the pre-writing phase
- the writing phase
- the post-writing phase.

Within each of these phases it is useful to focus, when appropriate, on one of the four aspects of written products described earlier: *ideas, organisation, language* or *mechanics*.

The pre-writing phase
The term pre-writing is used to mean all of the things writers do before they actually set pen to paper to begin the first draft. Firstly there is the choice of topic, and then the myriad of strategies which writers can use in rehearsing, planning, discussing, making notes and drawing diagrams before they plunge into commitment on paper. Of course, there are instances where spontaneity is better, especially during those rare flashes of inspiration which are experienced from time to time. But most of the writing which students do at school is enhanced by planning, and in fact, much of the hard slog of editing and refining at the end of a piece can be reduced if students are shown how to grapple with the problems beforehand. The act of writing becomes easier, more manageable and more satisfying, because students are less likely to need to make major changes to their drafts towards the end of the task, when energy and commitment may be waning.

Assessment of students' strategies at all stages of the writing process enables teachers to more accurately gauge and help students at the point of need rather than at the end of a piece of writing. Teachers' interventions can then be collaborative and enabling rather than judgemental.

In the pre-writing phase ideas for writing have not yet been fixed and the writer is free to play with alternatives. Teachers can help by recognising and providing support at the appropriate point, whether it be:
- the initial stage of considering possibilities
- the exploratory stage of collecting and connecting information and ideas
- the preparatory stage of making plans and rehearsing parts of what might eventually be put down on paper.

Where feasible, low profiency ESL students can be given support from parents or bilingual aides to do this in their home language.

Considering possibilities

At this point the focus may be almost completely on *ideas* or information. Attention is on topic choice, genre and purpose. The writer may engage in a range of activities such as:

- reflecting on personal interests, hobbies, sports, favourite people, places, issues
- brainstorming to generate ideas for topics
- browsing through past writings
- reading and listening to others read commercial, student made, or teacher made material
- discussing possibilities with peers, teacher, parents, bilingual aides, Aboriginal Education Worker (AEW), others
- thinking/reflecting on an idea/ideas
- making lists of possibilities
- thinking about the needs and interests of the reader
- searching through past lists of possibilities
- viewing television, videos
- listening to tapes
- drawing
- taping ideas.

Collecting and connecting

As the initial intention and purpose become clearer the writer may move into an exploratory phase, where topic choice is more or less decided, and the strategies for exploring possibilities around the topic become more apparent. Focus is probably still on ideas and information but perhaps issues of organisation, such as genre and format of final product also begin to appear.

At this stage strategies for gathering ideas and information might include:

- brainstorming, to tease out all the possible aspects of a chosen topic
- researching, which involves reading, interviewing, questioning, note taking, as well as using various resources such as books, pictures, films, tapes, newspapers to get a better idea of the scope of the topic, or to collect specific information
- formulating questions and answers
- drawing pictures
- reading or listening to someone read stories, poems, non-fiction, as models of the product they want to produce
- reviewing what they already know about the topic and what they want to find out
- selecting and re-reading appropriate material
- re-visiting past writings on similar subjects
- discussing any of the above with peers, teacher, parent, bilingual aide, AEW, others
- making jottings about any of this in a learning log or similar.

Organisational strategies at this point might include:
- deciding on topic, form or genre
- finding, examining models of the chosen form or genre
- collecting diagrams, charts, photographs
- planning illustrations.

Strategies to do with exploring the language of the particular piece might include:
- noticing the particular language of the models they are considering
- playing with language, for example creating metaphors, similes, examples
- experimenting with innovations on a structure, orally or in note form
- experimenting with appropriate styles ("Shall I write about it seriously, or will I try to make them laugh?").

Concerns about mechanics would probably be minimal at this exploratory stage, though the perfectionist, the superorganised or the anxious writer might be thinking about and finding out the spelling of key words, such as names of people and places.

Making plans and rehearsing parts

At some point in the pre-writing phase, exploring becomes more specific and focused, the task takes on a more definite structure, and the writer's activities become part of a rehearsal for the first draft. Now, as the ideas become more specific, the following strategies might be seen:
- refining, selecting, rejecting aspects of the ideas or information
- focusing on particular ideas and information
- making notes in a learning log
- drawing pictures more purposefully
- telling someone else (peers, teacher, parent, bilingual aide, AEW, other) about the ideas or information
- getting and considering feedback on the above.

As the ideas and information take shape and are refined and sorted, the writer's attention returns to organisational aspects of the writing:
- deciding on appropriate form or genre
- creating a structure, according to the form or genre chosen. If fiction, creating a storyline - setting the problem, goals, episodes, solutions and considering different beginning points. If non-fiction, selecting the information required and sorting it into suitable categories or sections. Perhaps also considering whether or not to write an index, glossary, introduction
- revisiting a model - specifically to note organisational details, and try out the structure, to see how well it fits the writer's intention. This might be done mentally, or orally, in discussion with peers, teacher, parent, AEW, bilingual aide or others
- jotting down plans, in writing or diagram form in learning log
- deciding what's missing and where it fits.

Throughout this rehearsal, the writer also experiments with the language appropriate for the particular piece of writing:
- mentally or orally rehearsing parts of the piece
- mentally, orally and possibly in writing, rehearsing and refining different leads
- mentally or orally comparing appropriate models of language with the intended product
- making notes about any of these in a learning log
- discussing any of the above with peers, teacher, parent, bilingual aide, AEW, others.

If much of the work on ideas, organisation and language has been tackled in the pre-writing phase, the writer is now in a better position to deal with issues of mechanics, which become more immediate in the actual writing phase of the process.

The writing phase
Writing begins at the point when a writer actually makes a start on a draft of the intended piece. For the purpose of focusing on strategies that writers can employ, it's useful to view writing as consisting of the two processes of drafting and revising.

The term "drafting" describes all the strategies used by writers to get their ideas down on paper in an ordered and coherent fashion for the intended audience. It may be approached in a range of ways by different writers, depending on their purposes and the amount of time spent in pre-writing preparation, but the two ends of the spectrum seem to be:
- a free writing approach whereby the writer lets the ideas flow freely in order to get them down on paper, and without giving deliberate attention to the constraints imposed by organisation, language and mechanics. This method has the advantage of releasing ideas in an uninterrupted flow, but is likely to require the writer to spend a considerable amount of time in revising the draft to meet the intentions and the audience's requirements
- a slower, but more considered approach, whereby the writer continually stops to re-read and revise throughout the drafting process. This method has the advantage that it may shorten the time spent in revising on completion of the draft.

The term "revising" describes all the strategies used by writers to review and change what is written in order to bring it closer to their intended outcomes. Revising may occur throughout the drafting process, as well as on the completion of a draft or drafts.

The strategies writers use to manage the complex processes of drafting and revising, have again been grouped under the headings which represent the main focus areas within a written product: ideas, organisation, language and mechanics. Because revising may occur throughout the drafting process, it's not appropriate to separate the strategies for the two processes.

Useful strategies for drafting and revising

The development of ideas can include some of the following strategies:
- referring to "pre-writing" notes, plans, drawings, etc
- writing freely to let ideas flow
- pausing to think and mentally rehearse what to say next
- drawing to help work out the development of ideas
- acting out the ideas represented so far to develop them further
- talking to others about what to say/asking for help
- seeking additional information
- re-reading for clarity of ideas and general sense
- seeking reaction/feedback to the ideas/information
- considering questions about the ideas posed by others
- adding/deleting information, giving examples, clarifying points, giving specific details.

Organisation of a piece of writing can involve:
- referring to "pre-writing" notes, plans, diagrams, etc
- pausing to think about the organisation of the piece
- talking to others about the organisation of the piece
- checking to see if the organisation conforms to the structure for that particular form of writing
- re-reading for logical sequence, linking of ideas, effect of opening and conclusion
- seeking reaction/feedback from others to the way ideas are presented
- marking in paragraphs, headings, sections, pages, illustrations
- using arrows, carets, asterisks, cutting and pasting to re-structure
- using a word processor to reorganise the piece.

Language use in a piece of writing can involve the writer in:
- referring to pre-writing lists of words, phrases, etc.
- stopping to mentally or orally rehearse the best way of wording something
- drawing to generate or sustain language
- seeking additional information about vocabulary and syntax from models, other resources or other people
- checking for conformity when using language models
- re-reading for improvements in choice of words, suitability of grammatical usage, general sense
- checking to see that sentences flow, that there is a balance between sentence types and a consistency in tone
- checking to avoid inappropriate repetitions
- referring to language usage check-lists
- reading aloud to see how it sounds
- listening to others read it aloud, or a taped version, to see how it sounds.

The mechanics of writing can be handled by:
- proof reading for omissions, repetitions, misspellings, punctuation
- reading aloud for punctuation
- circling temporary spellings
- checking temporary spellings from a variety of sources
- having others proof read
- referring to checklists for proof reading
- checking legibility, use of spaces, general layout
- rewriting for legibility
- using a word processor
- dictating to a scribe.

The post-writing phase
In the post-writing phase the writer decides either to:
- continue no further with the product, or
- publish the product for the intended audience.

If the decision is made to continue no further, the piece of writing is simply recorded as part of the student's range of writing experiences and then filed.

If the decision is to publish, the following processes can be considered:
- preparing for publishing
- presenting to the intended audience and reflecting on responses.

Preparing for publishing

The term "publishing" is used in the broad sense to cover the range of ways in which different forms of writing are presented for their intended audiences. As students prepare their writing for publishing, their focus will now be entirely on mechanics. Teachers might observe how students:
- proofread - checking spelling, punctuation and grammar
- talk to others about publishing ideas
- examine other published work
- choose materials for inclusion such as photographs, diagrams
- arrange the layout, by hand or on a word processor
- decide on details of the format, such as type size, print styles
- prepare illustrations
- translate home language into English.

Presenting to the audience and reflecting on responses

Depending on the particular kind of writing, students may:
- display the book, project, poem in an appropriate place - library, classroom, home
- post the letter
- read aloud to the intended audience
- rehearse and perform the piece.

Teachers might then note how students reflect on their audience's reactions in terms of:

- how clearly the message was received
- aspects the audience particularly enjoyed
- aspects which needed further clarification
- what the writer might do next time.

CAASR : ATTITUDES TO READING

The energy source which fuels the act of reading is the reader's engagement with the task of making meaning from the text. Influences which affect this engagement are the reader's:

- self concept with regard to reading
- commitment to investing thought, time and energy in the task.

Teachers need to know about these in order to provide classroom contexts and climates which nurture young readers and provide them with the support and encouragement they need.

Self-concept

If teachers want to find out how students feel about themselves as readers, and how different tasks, purposes and types of texts affect these feelings, then they need to find ways of monitoring and recording:

- the circumstances in which students anticipate reading with a sense of pleasure, achievement and satisfaction
- students' use of reading as a means of illuminating, clarifying, organising and raising questions about aspects of their world
- the extent to which students use reading for their own purposes.

Commitment

Teachers can find out about students' willingness to:

- take risks, e.g. choose books they are interested in even though the texts may be a little more difficult; tackle a wide variety of familiar and unfamiliar books
- assume responsibility for choice of reading matter, for setting their own purposes, for accepting or rejecting particular texts for particular purposes
- change books if the text does not meet their needs or expectations
- ask for help and advice from peers, teacher, librarian, AEW, bilingual aide
- accept uncertainty, suspend judgement, allow the author a little scope and time before rejecting a text
- ignore distractions and stay on task
- share their reading with others and discuss insights, opinions, interpretations, visual imagery
- be critically reflective and use their own knowledge and experiences to compare, illuminate and enrich texts
- read in home language as well as in English.

Teachers also need to find out about the possible range of positive and negative influences on students' self-esteem and commitment which may include:
- lower expectations based on racial and gender stereotyping
- poverty
- sexual, racial and other forms of harassment
- attitudes to disability
- recency of migration and of learning English
- history of success in learning
- acknowledgement and valuing of students' experiences, culture and language
- range of books available in the student's home language.

CAASR : ASPECTS OF READING COMPREHENSION

When writers create texts (pieces of writing of any kind) they select from their store of information about the world and the particular topic a particular set of understandings they wish to share with their readers. The central focus in the assessment of reading ought then to be on students' success in re-creating the understandings the writer intended.

Sometimes this understanding demands exactness of re-creation. For example, a reader faced with the task of defusing a time-bomb can ill-afford to misinterpret the written directions for this task. Similarly, the new intern checking to find out the correct dose of medication for an ailment has to attend to the text very closely.

With other kinds of texts, understanding does not rely on exact re-creation. Readers of fantasy novels or romances have plenty of scope to interpret details of the experience described, in the light of their own wishes or experience. They create understandings within certain boundaries and they are able to fill out the picture in their own way.

Because different texts and different purposes involve different levels of processing information there are different ways of checking whether students are reading successfully. "Comprehension scores" on reading tests provide very limited information because reading test passages and then rereading them to answer test questions, is a very specialised kind of reading.

Reading a favourite novel is a different kind of reading. One way parents know that it is being successfully performed is when their children insist on staying up late to read in bed. They know the children are engaging with the experience of the book. Similarly, when teachers see students reading eagerly in class or excitedly sharing the experience of a book with their friends, they know that these students are succeeding in making sense of the book.

Reading reference works for information is different again. Students' ability to use particular texts can be checked by asking them to find out specific pieces of information. For example, students reveal a particular level of competence when they can skim a recipe and tell how much vinegar is to be used.

With other reading tasks it may be more appropriate to check students' understanding by asking them to reveal their own interpretation of what they have read. For example, they may be asked to retell what happened or explain why a character behaved in a particular way.

Such commonsense comprehension checks have the virtue that they suit the purposes students have for reading. For it is purpose that determines the extent to which readers re-create the understandings that the writer intended. When students really want to achieve something from print they will often overcome considerable difficulties. On the contrary when they have little reason for reading or no real commitment to a reading task they may read carelessly and teachers' checks on comprehension may reveal very little of the potential they have.

While purpose and commitment are important factors affecting comprehension, the success that students have in understanding what they read is also critically affected by the match between what they know about ideas and information, text organisation, language and mechanics and what the writer of the particular text expects them to know.

Ideas and information

Topic knowledge

At the heart of the process of making sense of authors' intended messages is the reader's ability to make connections between what she/he knows and what the author is writing about. The more familiar the reader is with the topic, the easier it is to make these connections.

Knowledge of the world

Writers quite properly assume their readers will have knowledge of the world and do not bother to tell their readers what they already know. For example, a novelist writing about a scene in a restaurant assumes that readers will know what goes on in restaurants - that diners are shown to the table, offered menus, etc. and then when they leave they pay, perhaps with a tip. Readers who have had experience of restaurants or who have learned about them through film and television will understand what the writer intended. Readers who do not have such knowledge of the world or who have had different cultural experiences may find it difficult to reconstruct the meanings the writer intended. It may be useful, therefore, to watch for occasions when students' success in reading is affected by the mismatch between their experience and the experience the writer assumes.

Organisation
Successful readers use what they know about text organisation to predict and check their hypotheses about the sequence of texts and about the relationships between the parts.

Fiction

Teachers can look for evidence that students know about the typical features of fiction:
- the setting
- the problem
- the episodes
- the resolution or outcome
- the conclusion.

Non-fiction

They can look at students' use of the organisational features of non-fiction texts:
- titles
- headings
- sub-headings
- chapters
- contents
- index
- glossaries
- page numbers.

They can look for evidence of students' awareness of the particular structures of non-fiction texts such as:
- explanations
- reports
- descriptions
- arguments
- instructions
- directions
- alphabetical listings
- numerical listings.

Focus and sequence

Other aspects to look for are the students' awareness of:
- the focus of what they read: *can they summarise what the text is about?*
- the sequence of the whole text and the relationship between the parts.

Language
Two critical aspects of students' ability to understand texts are their knowledge of the meanings and relationships signalled by the syntax of the language and their understanding of the meanings signalled by words.

Syntax

Teachers need to monitor students' reading to find out:
- what kinds of sentences they find easy or difficult:
  e.g. Some students may not detect the change in meaning of these
     two sentences:
  "John hit Mary."
  "John was hit by Mary."

Word meanings

- students' understanding of the way in which common words take
  on different meanings according to the way in which they are used:
  e.g. "There was a run on the bank."
       "They had to run home."
       "The printer did a small run of pamphlets."

Teachers will need to be aware that the home languages of NESB
students may not have equivalent words and meanings for those they
find in English.

Style
Furthermore teachers can find out about students' awareness of the
following aspects of style in the texts they read:
- the stance of the writer (humorous, serious, pleading, satirical)
- how the writer builds up atmosphere and its effect on the reader
- use of dialogue and dialect
- the precise vocabulary the writer uses for the topic of the text.

Students' awareness of these aspects will be influenced by cultural and
linguistic factors. An example of this is the difficulty of interpreting a
writer's humorous intentions across cultures.

Mechanics
Frequently this is the area which receives the greatest attention in
reading assessment but, as can be seen from the assessment
framework, this is only one of four kinds of information that readers
must use in order to be successful. What then are the kinds of
information which need monitoring in this area?

Letter-sound relationships

- the particular sounds of English language
- the letters used for representing sounds/meanings
- the relationship between letters and sounds
- the range of forms letters can take (e.g. capitals, lower case, print,
  italics, cursive, etc.).

Directional and positional
conventions

- across a letter, a word, a sentence, a whole book
- top to bottom of a page
- front to back of a book
- spaces mark word boundaries.

Punctuation conventions	<ul><li>full stops</li><li>capital letters</li><li>commas, apostrophes, colons, semi-colons</li><li>exclamation marks</li><li>question marks</li><li>hyphens</li><li>speech marks.</li></ul>
Devices for showing emphasis or importance	<ul><li>underlining</li><li>italics</li><li>bold face type</li><li>larger type.</li></ul>
Layout conventions	<ul><li>pagination</li><li>indenting of paragraphs</li><li>conventions for noting</li><li>relationship between pictures and texts</li><li>spacing</li><li>headings.</li></ul>

Later chapters show the many different ways for assessing students' success in reading. With experienced readers the responses they make are reliable demonstrations of their understanding of particular texts. With young readers who are still grappling with working out words particular attention will need to be paid to the understandings they have and the strategies they use to make sense of text.

CAASR : STRATEGIES FOR READING

There are four categories of reading strategies used by readers: basic, monitoring for congruence, creating worlds and coping.

Basic strategies

For proficient readers, reading is, in a sense, "natural". People easily process a lot of print in the environment because they know what to expect. They attend to just enough graphic detail to determine what information is presented. Young students do the same with signs and labels before they know much about letters and words.

This process of predicting on the basis of what is known, sampling just enough text to confirm predictions (or rereading and sampling further if the predictions are not confirmed) is a feature of proficient reading too.

These basic strategies are what teachers hope to see students using. Therefore they will want to monitor students' reading to see how they predict, check, confirm and/or self-correct. Teachers may notice how students:

Predict	Predict such things as:

Predict such things as:
- the kind of text
- what sort of information the author may deal with
- the connections between ideas
- the outcomes
- the next word, phrase, sentence or sequence of ideas.

Confirm and check

Confirm and check such things as:
- what the author means
- what a word is
- the visual details of letters and words
- the pronunciation of words
- sentence structure
- the meaning of words.

Self-correct

Self-correct on the basis of:
- what makes sense
- what sounds right
- what looks right.

For example, students who are reading for meaning expect that the language they "hear" as they read will be made up of words and sentences that sound right. If it doesn't they may:
- hesitate
- read on to see if they can solve the problem
- reread
- substitute or delete words
- self-correct.

Monitoring for congruence
Good readers go beyond the monitoring of language to monitor the ideas and information that the text presents. They expect that what they understand will be congruent with:
- what they have read so far in the text
- what they, themselves, know about the world.

For example, students engaged with the experience of a story will be concerned if a character, previously depicted as good natured, suddenly and inexplicably behaves in a mean and nasty manner. Their response will be of the kind, *What's going on here?* In a similar way students will be concerned when they encounter behaviour or information that seriously conflicts with what they already know about the world. Their response will be of the kind, *That can't be right!*

Evidence of such critical monitoring of the ideas and information of what students read is made available when they are encouraged to share their responses to reading, and to talk seriously about how the ideas and information relate to their own experience.

Students' gender and cultural background will have an important influence on what they know about the world and how they experience it, so that teachers can expect differences in how and what students determine is congruent.

Creating worlds

Good readers are able to be critically responsive to certain kinds of text because they become involved in the world of the text. More precisely, they create, with the help of cues provided by the writer, a partly imagined world. As they read they become "lost" in the time and place of the story. In a sense they engage in the experience of the story, inhabiting the setting, taking part in the action and experiencing the emotions of characters.

One way to learn about how students are engaging in the experience of stories is to ask them how they visualise the setting, the events, and the characters in their reading. From minimal cues provided by the writer readers can inhabit rich settings, live with complex characters, take part in complicated events and experience a range of powerful emotions. To have a "window" in this world of created experience is to understand how rewarding reading can be for students.

Coping strategies

Good readers, even at an early age, develop powerful strategies for making some sense of difficult texts that require more knowledge and experience than they currently possess. These strategies almost invariably involve students drawing on what they already know so that they can work out what is new. So they can draw on:
• ideas: what they already know about the topic and about the world and what is new
• organisation: what they already know about the way texts can be organised and what is unfamiliar
• language: which words and sentences do make sense to them and what causes difficulty
• mechanics: the words they know and the ones which need to be looked at closely.

Experienced teachers know that students are helped to make sense of difficult text when they:
• focus on what they already know about the topic
• try to work out the way in which the ideas and information are organised
• try to translate difficult language into simple language that they understand

- use a variety of context and within-word cues to work out what a word may be.

Specific strategies may include:
- writing down what is already known
- talking with others about the topic
- getting information from simple books and other media
- using diagrams, outlines, etc.
- getting someone to read the passage aloud
- skim reading to get an overall idea of organisation (headings, subheadings, numbering) etc.
- rereading the whole or parts
- breaking into parts
- picking out key words and key sentences
- making a diagram of ideas or information
- making an outline or a summary
- reading aloud
- underlining difficult words
- reading on to work out what words might mean
- reading on to get sufficient context to identify words
- comparing words or parts with known words
- breaking words into syllables or sound segments.

Of course one of the most important skills readers can develop is the ability to recognise that a particular text may require knowledge and experience so far beyond what the reader has that it makes sense to reject the text and seek some other source of information. Often, however, once the reader has built up the necessary store of knowledge, a previously inaccessible text becomes readable.

Students need to be taught such strategies for coping with difficult texts. The ways in which they use them can easily be monitored through observation, talking with them and reading their accounts of how they operate.

CAASR : RANGE OF STUDENTS' READING AND WRITING
In literate cultures written language can be used to do many things, and it can take many different forms. A range of written language uses is given on page 9 in the section "Concepts about literacy."

Teachers need to provide students with situations which expose them to as much of this range as possible, in order to extend their experiences in reading and writing. Learning is more effective when students are encouraged to write and read for a variety of real-life purposes and to write for real audiences. Students' intentions for reading and writing determine the kinds of outcomes that occur.

By keeping track of the different purposes which students have for writing, teachers can ensure that a reasonable balance of writing forms is also tried.

Similarly records of the texts read provide teachers with useful information about students' choices and interests, as well as the quantity of material read over a given period.

Teachers need to monitor the range of:
- topics the student chooses to read and write about
- purposes and audiences the student writes for
- kinds of reading and writing the student engages in
- purposes for reading
- use of home language for reading and writing.

CAASR : WRITING OVERVIEW

CONCEPTS ABOUT LITERACY
Uses for written language
Kinds of written products
The possible range of audiences
The appropriate use of written language
The similarities and differences between speech and writing
The processes readers and writers use

ATTITUDES TO WRITING
Self Concept
Commitment

ASPECTS OF WRITTEN PRODUCTS
Ideas/Information
Topic knowledge
Knowledge of the world
Presentation of ideas
Organisation
Kinds of writing
Focus
Parts
Sequences
Links
Readers' needs
Language
Vocabulary
Sentences
Style
Mechanics
Handwriting
Spelling
Punctuation
Layout
Using word processors

STRATEGIES FOR WRITING
Pre-writing
Considering possibilities
Collecting and connecting
Making plans and rehearsing parts
Writing
Drafting
Revising
Post-writing
Preparing for publishing
Presenting to the audience and reflecting on responses

RANGE OF STUDENTS' READING AND WRITING

CAASR : READING OVERVIEW

CONCEPTS ABOUT LITERACY
Uses for written language
Kinds of written products
The possible range of audiences
The appropriate use of written language
The similarities and differences between speech and writing
The processes readers and writers use

ATTITUDES TO READING
Self Concept
Commitment

ASPECTS OF READING COMPREHENSION
Ideas/Information
Topic knowledge
Knowledge of the world
Organisation
Fiction texts
Non-fiction texts
Focus and sequence
Language
Syntax
Word meanings
Style
Mechanics
Letter-sound relationships
Directional & positional conventions
Punctuation conventions
Devices for showing emphasis or importance
Layout conventions

STRATEGIES FOR READING
Basic strategies
Predict
Confirm and check
Self correct
Monitoring for congruence
Creating worlds
Coping strategies

RANGE OF STUDENTS' READING AND WRITING

4   COLLECTING INFORMATION

This chapter identifies six ways of gathering information about students' learning:
- administering tests
- analysing students' reading outcomes and writing products
- observing reading and writing behaviours
- student/teacher interactions
- drawing on student record-keeping and self-assessment
- collecting information from parents and others.

Each of these is described in terms of:
- type of information likely to be obtained
- opportunities which already exist, or which you can can create, for using this technique
- organisational factors to be considered
- constraints.

The chart on p.84 provides an overview of this chapter. The information you collect will be guided by your own questions and concerns about the students in your classroom, and the specific purpose you have in mind at the time, in regard to your program. Deciding on your focus beforehand and selecting the most appropriate information gathering technique will ensure that your assessment procedure is effective and time-efficient.

ADMINISTERING TESTS
As a teacher you check all the time to see what your students can do, how they go about their tasks, what they achieve, and what they struggle with. For the most part, you do not need to use formal tests, because every act of reading and writing is a test, in that it provides information about what students can do, which tasks they succeed with and the kinds of strategies they use.

Occasionally, however, you may wish to conduct a quick spelling test or dictation to check on specific aspects of writing. Or you may design a "comprehension" test to check whether students have attended to, or understood, specific information in a passage.

Of course teaching would be much easier, though less interesting, if you could get published tests of reading and writing that could tell you what your students could do as readers and writers, how they operated, what their achievements were, and what they struggled with.

Unfortunately published tests simply cannot fulfil all these purposes. They can however be used to obtain information about quite specific aspects of the CAASR framework, particularly in regard to the mechanics of reading and writing. They also have some limited use as screening devices.

Opportunities for administering tests
Opportunities for using this information collecting technique involve:
- using published tests of writing
- using published tests of reading
- using teacher made tests of reading and writing.

Using published writing tests

In 1988 teachers in the Literacy and Learning in the Middle Years (LLIMY) and AWRITE projects surveyed the use of tests in some fifty State, Catholic and Independent schools. The compiled results showed that, apart from spelling tests in upper primary grades, there were few, if any, published writing tests in use. It seems that South Australian teachers are happy to assess student writing on the basis of what they write as part of the usual curriculum.

However, the published tests which are used are mainly tests of spelling and are often administered at the beginning of the year in an attempt to provide an idea of the range of student performance.

The better tests include a scheme for analysing each student's errors so you have information to direct the help you give individual students. Still, once you have a scheme for analysing errors (*Spelling : R-7 Language Arts*, Education Department of South Australia, 1984, pp.32-33) you do not really need a test. In the end you are likely to get more information about your students' spelling from the tests you design yourself (*Spelling : R-7 Language Arts*, Education Department of South Australia, 1984, pp.38-40).

Using published reading tests

The previously mentioned survey of testing in fifty schools revealed that a handful of published reading tests were being used for a variety of purposes. The most common purpose was to find out about the range of reading performance at a particular year level.

Any of these published reading tests provide only a very rough estimate of performance because they sample only a narrow range of reading behaviours. For example these tests may focus on any *one* of the following:

1. The ability to read isolated words (e.g. Schonell R1 Graded Reading Vocabulary Test or the St. Lucia Graded Word Reading Test). Reading words in isolation is a task that bears little resemblance to normal reading and can, in fact, be more difficult for inexperienced readers than reading coherent text.

2. The ability to guess the exact words left out of sentences (e.g. GAPADOL or St. Lucia Comprehension Test). Often trying to guess the word to fit the slot becomes a problem solving task more difficult than normal reading.

3. The ability to answer questions about a passage of text. A major problem with this kind of test is that students can often answer the questions correctly without even understanding what the passages are about. A further problem is that, in order to reduce cultural and experiential bias, the test designers produce passages which are remote from everyone's experience and thus constitute an unreal reading task.

Such tests may still have some limited use as quick screening devices that must be followed up by a more detailed assessment of reading behaviour.

While properly administered standardised norm-referenced tests may be useful as a rough screening device, they are not designed to provide a measure of reading progress. At best they indicate how a student's performance on the particular test on one occasion compares with the performance of a sample of students the same age. The tests bear little relation to the reading program the student experiences and so scores from a test taken later in the year often measure test-taking skills as much as progress in the reading program. The exception, of course, are those schools in the United States where the reading program becomes instruction in the narrow range of skills needed to pass standardised reading tests.

The critical question then that you need to ask yourself is: *What exactly are these tests testing and how much can I conclude from the scores they provide?*

Some reading tests avoid the problems of norm-referenced tests designed to compare students' performance with sample populations. These other tests allow you to see what students can do and are often referred to as "criterion-referenced" tests. Published tests of this kind claim to have a diagnostic purpose such as finding out whether a student can read sentences with phonically regular words:

e.g. Has a top a lid?
      Can a dog sip?

The problem is that they cover only a narrow range of so-called "skills" – usually only knowledge of letter-sound relationships which constitute just one part (albeit an important part) of the information that students need to succeed as readers.

Published reading tests almost invariably have a strong bias towards the middle range of the dominant culture. This counts against NESB readers and must be taken into account when selecting tests.

Using teacher made tests of reading and writing

You are likely to find that the criterion-referenced tests you make yourself – quick checks to see that the students can do what you expect – are much more useful. For example you can ask students to:
- read a passage aloud
- talk about something they have read silently
- read for specific information
- read a story to find out what a character did next, who got the prize, etc.

By varying texts and reading tasks (e.g. including "how" and "why" questions) you allow students to show you a wide range of achievements in reading. For some students, particularly those with language delays, it may be appropriate to ask them to retell the text. For other students it may be more appropriate to ask "how" and "why" questions.

The writing tests you make yourself will usually focus on some aspects of writing such as spelling, punctuation or handwriting. However, the best "test" of these things is what students do in their everyday writing across the curriculum.

Organising to administer reading/writing tests
To ensure testing is carried out in an efficient and effective manner you will need to:
- consider carefully what you want to find out and why, and then select or devise a test which best suits your purposes
- decide when you will have students do the test and take into account how you will deal with student absences, interruptions, etc. which may occur
- plan time for marking, recording, scoring and analysing test results.

Constraints of this assessment practice
You need to confront the fact that no published test can (or ever will) provide you with the comprehensive, detailed information that you need in order to assess your students' performance in reading and writing. At best, published tests provide a rough check, another source of information, on the broader assessment that you yourself make. Most published tests are so limited in their scope and purpose, and so liable to misinterpretation, that they will never provide a satisfactory alternative to the comprehensive, balanced and equitable assessment program that you can devise.

Most of the tests that are norm-referenced (i.e. that allow you to compare your students with a national sample) are designed to get a spread of results. To do this they include almost impossibly difficult or tricky questions. So the tests become tests of confidence, experience, reasoning and problem solving abilities as well as tests of reading.

Experienced test takers learn to overcome these problems. They learn to re-read passages or read the questions before the passage. Some of the most successful learn answers off by heart because they have had the same test so many times.

Not only are there very definite constraints on the value of tests to determine what students can do, there are also very severe constraints on how you can use the results of published tests, particularly those that give "reading ages" or "spelling ages." Nobody has a "reading age." All you can say is that a student has achieved a score on a narrow range of reading tasks that can be compared with a sample of other students' scores on the same tasks. The rough score does not say anything about what books a student is able to read or how well the student processes text to get particular information. So the practice of trying to match the so-called "reading ages" of students with the so-called "reading ages" of books is pointless hard work. There is no necessary relation between a student's score on a norm-referenced test and the "readability" score of a book (normally derived from measures of familiar words and complex sentences).

The practice of using "reading and spelling ages" as the basis for "ability" grouping is totally ineffective because students who score the same "age" simply do not have the same needs as readers and writers. To group them together then and provide them with similar instruction does not foster their learning.

Some students may be disadvantaged in test situations because of disabilities eg: hearing and sight problems. Such disabilities may prevent them from doing what is required.

Similarly, timed tests may also disadvantage students with co-ordination problems, handwriting problems, or students who work at a much slower and more deliberate pace than others.

One of the most distressing things about published tests is the way their supposedly "objective" and authoritative nature encourages teachers to ignore their own assessments and judgements about individual students. This is highlighted by a report from a 10 year old student's parents who were shocked to find that their son, a highly successful reader and writer, was assigned to a special class to do phonics exercises. It appeared that testing a month before had revealed "problems." When the matter was investigated the principal found that the test scores had been "mixed up" and the boy wrongly assigned to the special class, but the teacher who knew him didn't challenge the findings of the test.

The conclusion you are left with is that for all their appearance of objectivity publishers' tests are no substitute for the commonsense information that you can get in the ways suggested in the following sections.

ANALYSING STUDENTS' READING OUTCOMES AND WRITING PRODUCTS

Tests usually provide information about fragments of a student's literacy development (e.g. word recognition, knowledge of letters and sounds). More varied and detailed evidence of your students' growth as readers and writers can be found by analysing the work they produce as part of their daily learning experiences across the curriculum.

During any week your students create a range of writing products and reading outcomes in response to the tasks you set. These take a variety of forms:
- notes, diagrams, plans for writing
- written products across the curriculum (stories, poems, reports, summaries, reviews, projects)
- spelling lists
- written outcomes from reading (review comments, answers to questions, research notes, etc.)
- other outcomes from reading (drawings, dramatisations, models, etc.)
- student's self-evaluative writing (journals, reflection books, learning logs).

When viewed collectively, these products and outcomes enable you to monitor the range of literacy experiences the student has engaged in. This process is essential to effective programming as it enables you to ensure that you are setting tasks that will develop all the areas of reading and writing that are outlined in the CAASR framework (see Chapter 3).

The individual products and outcomes of these tasks can then be analysed with a particular focus in mind, e.g. "What does this piece of writing show about the students' revising strategies?"

Below are some examples of the kind of information this technique can provide.

Notes, diagrams, plans for writing

By looking at the written plans or drawings students make before they write you may discover information about their use of gathering and organisational strategies in the pre-writing stage.

Some teachers organise for students to keep all notes, diagrams and plans for writing in one book called a "learning log" (Calkins, 1986). This means they are easily accessible for analysis. The example below is taken from a student's learning log and shows his exploration of four possible ideas for a writing project.

Some of the things it shows about the student's use of pre-writing strategies are that he:
- draws on personal experience for writing topics
- distinguishes between fiction and fact in writing
- uses drawings to help focus ideas
- brainstorms words and phrases to use in writing.

This planning may also reveal the writer's awareness of particular aspects of that type of writing. For example, a student who has jotted down information in chronological order as planning for a biography is showing awareness that this is how biographies are often organised.

Written products — drafts and final versions

A great deal of information can be found out about students' use of strategies and their knowledge of aspects of written products by looking at their drafts and final products from a range of curriculum areas.

The draft below was produced when students were set the task of researching the topic "Egyptian Pyramids" in order to prepare a brief written report for their classmates. Depending on what the teacher wants to find out, this draft can be analysed for information about several aspects of the student's reading and writing.

Ancient
Egyptian Pyramids 24/9/98

~~The pyramids~~ All Scientists beleve nearly "all" pyramids were made between 2664 and 2180 BC. They are made with limestone and sand stone which egyptions cut with ~~useia~~ a copper saws and pulled the blocks using sledges ropes & and levers. Pyramids were built & with steps up and a flat top so temples ~~who~~ were able to join on to it. Scholars think egptians thought that the shape of the pyramid has a religious meaning The biggest ever pyamid is the Knufu at Gizos (origanally) 147m high. It contains 2,300,000 2.5 ton lime and sand stone blocks all pulled by egyptians. The second famous pyramid ~~is~~ was built by (acreir) egyptions for their rolers or pharaohs. Indians have also built pyramids in Mexico, Central and South America, but with most case the pyramids were not fort (burial) reasons. There are now only thirty-five ruins are standing.

In this case, the teacher was particularly interested in seeing how the student organised the information, and noted that he:
- used an appropriate beginning and concluding sentence
- related information to the central focus of "pyramids"
- ordered information in a logical and coherent way.

While recognising these achievements, the teacher also noted that the student needed to be introduced to the use of:
- paragraphs for ordering different parts
- an introduction to outline the scope of the report
- a conclusion to summarise the main points.

The draft can also be examined for what it shows about the student's knowledge of the appropriate ideas, language or mechanics for report writing.

The changes made to the draft provide some evidence of the student's use of drafting and revising strategies. It can be seen that he:
- has changed the first words for a more effective beginning
- self-corrects while drafting
- makes insertions
- circles unknown spellings.

This kind of task, which involved the students in reading information, can also show how effectively the student was able to make sense of the relevant information. In the report on "Egyptian Pyramids" the fact that the student has presented the information so simply and coherently seems to suggest a reasonable understanding of the source material.

The written products of young students may consist of only a few letters or words, but these can still provide a great deal of evidence of their development. An example of a proforma for recording teachers' analysis of writing is included in Appendix 5 (a). Some examples of detailed analyses of written products, including those of young students, are included in Appendix 5 (b,c,d).

Spelling lists

When students keep lists of the words which they need when writing, these lists provide some evidence of the kinds of spelling issues which each student is addressing. One teacher and her students devised the following format for the students to keep track of their spelling needs and achievements:

		"Have a go Jo!" sheet	Name:	
			Class:	
Date	My Try (Look how close I was!)	Checked with	Correct Spelling
9/9	likt	Mrs. D	liked
19/9	Mcdonlds	wall chart	Mc donalds
20/9	Mikl	Michael	Michael
26/9	jumped	Mrs. D	✓

- in the example the student's *My Try* list can be analysed in relation to other knowledge about the student. It may show that she is: using sound/symbol relationships to attempt unknown words (Mikl); exploring the use of the suffix "ed" (likt, jumped); using capital letters for names (Mcdonlds, Mikl)
- the *Checked with* column provides information about the resources the student uses to check spelling
- looking at the growing list of words provides an overview of the range of words the student is attempting.

The spelling errors and self-corrections students make in their drafts can also be analysed for evidence of development. (Refer to *Spelling: R-7 Language Arts* pp.32-37.)

Students' reading outcomes

From written responses to reading such as review comments, retellings and answers to focus questions you can find out about your students' comprehension of specific aspects of texts, such as their awareness of character, setting and plot within a fictional text's organisation. Many teachers are finding students' written retellings of their reading a useful source of information. They use the following procedure suggested by Brown and Cambourne (1987).

• look at the text title and predict what it will be about
• list some words which might be in the text
• listen to the text read aloud while reading own copy silently
• reread as often as needed
• retell the text in own words.

From monitoring the students' engagement in each of these steps and analysing the written retelling, teachers can find out about the students':

• background knowledge about the topic
• use of strategies such as predicting, rereading for sense, etc.
• vocabulary knowledge and spelling competencies
• understandings of the ideas, organisation, language and mechanics of the text.

Some responses, particularly the students' review comments or personal reactions, will add to your insights into such aspects as types of reading they are interested in and why, which aspects of texts they particularly enjoy, reasons for losing interest.

The following is a student's note to the teacher explaining why she would like to postpone reading her current book. The students in this class refer to this as "rain chequing" (R.C.) the book.

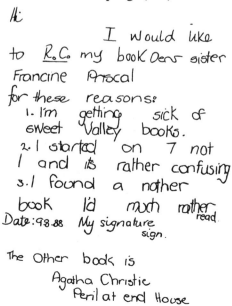

Hi

I would like to R.C. my book Dens sister Francine Pascal for these reasons:
1. I'm getting sick of Sweet Valley books.
2. I started on 7 not 1 and its rather confusing
3. I found a nother book I'd much rather read.
Date: 98.88 My signature sign.

The other book is
Agatha Christie
Peril at end House

It shows that she:
- is able to provide considered reasons for rejecting a book
- has chosen to try another type of fiction
- has discovered that reading "series" books out of sequence can affect understanding.

Further information about students' use of strategies to make sense of the text and to visualise the world of the book can be elicited by asking them to respond to questions such as:

"Does this character remind you of anyone you know?"

"Can you describe the way you are seeing this scene?"

(See Appendix 6 for examples of focus questions.)

You can ask your students to respond to reading in ways other than writing, such as drawing, model making or dramatisation.

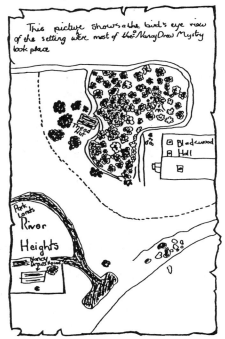

This picture shows a the bird's eye view of the setting were most of the Nancy Drew Mystry book place

The outcomes of these activities can also provide you with evidence of development. For example:
- a student's dramatisation of an episode from a novel or picture book may show an understanding of the underlying theme represented by the ideas
- students' creation of a play about everyday life but using a plot from their reading demonstrates that they are making sense of what they read through their personal experiences
- a series of drawings depicting the main events of a story shows that the student is aware of the organisation of the plot

- a model or drawing of a scene from a story may reveal both an understanding of the organisational features of setting and the student's use of creating strategies to visualise the scene.

Students' written self-assessments

This type of writing and the information it provides is fully discussed later in this chapter under the technique of "Drawing on student record-keeping and self-assessment", pp.66-76.

Some opportunities for analysing reading outcomes and writing products are next explored, as well as organisational factors and constraints of this technique.

Opportunities for analysing reading outcomes and writing products

Some opportunities for analysing students' work occur:
- while students are doing reading and writing tasks
- during reading and writing conferences
- after collecting samples of students' work.

While students are doing reading and writing tasks

You can pick up information about students' writing simply by looking over their shoulders as they are engaged in tasks, especially when they're encouraged to share parts of their work with you as you move around the room. For example you may notice that a student has included the clause, "the murky clouds blotted out the light", in the opening paragraph of a ghost story. This is an ideal opportunity to note the vivid use of language and give immediate feedback on this achievement.

When outcomes to reading tasks involve some form of presentation, as in the case of a play, an oral retelling, or a display of artwork, those may also be occasions when you can note evidence of new development and give feedback "on the spot".

During reading and writing conferences

When time is scheduled to see students in individual or group conferences, you can spend part of that time reading and commenting on the particular aspects of the writing product or reading outcome which are the subject of the conference. Because of time constraints it is best if individual conferences take only a few minutes. It is therefore necessary to concentrate on monitoring development in only one or two chosen aspects in any one conference (e.g. character development and linking of paragraphs in a science fiction story).

Collecting samples of students' work

There are times when you will do a thorough analysis of a piece of work in which you focus on several features at once and note achievements and teaching points. This will involve you in making decisions about what information you want to discover and which type of work will best provide it. You will then need to collect the selected sample and keep it until the analysis is completed. For instance you may collect one sample of a student's fiction and non-fiction writing each term and write detailed feedback on the ideas, organisation, language and mechanics of each piece. This type of analysis requires more time and concentration than is normally possible in a busy classroom so you may need to either organise uninterrupted class time, or be prepared to allocate non instructional time or after hours time.

Organising for analysis of writing products and reading outcomes
To make analysis of students' writing products and reading outcomes an efficient assessment technique you will need to organise for it to happen. Some ways to do this are:

- Plan times both in and out of the classroom in which work can be read and analysed. For instance you can allocate the first ten minutes of writing or reading sessions to spend moving around the room and reading parts of students' work "in progress". Non-instructional time, or the time while students are engaged in other tasks or eating their lunches, can also be used. You can roster reading and writing conferences so that you are able to spend a few minutes each week analysing work with each student.
- Collect samples of work from only a few students each week to keep the task of analysing them manageable.
- Work out in advance exactly what you want to find out from the analysis so that you have a clear and manageable focus. How many aspects you can attend to in any piece will depend on the time available.
- Make students aware of the criteria you are using and as much as possible involve them in the process of analysis. This may mean helping them to construct sets of guidelines to follow for particular types of writing which they can then use to comment on how successfully the finished product meets these recommendations. (An example of a student devised list of guidelines for editing can be seen in the section on "Drawing on student record-keeping and self-assessment" pp.66-76).

You can organise for students coming to a writing conference to have already written their own comments about the ideas, organisation, language or mechanics of their writing. A check-list of questions about these aspects can be a useful guide. (See example in Appendix 7.) Alternatively you might provide them with a special sheet to comment on, such as the one shown on the next page.

- Work out efficient ways for you and the students to record the most important aspects of the analysis. Some teachers set up a section of the students' "Record Books" (see description of students' record books in chapter 5 on "Storing information") for students to record their own comments and feedback from others.

SELF ASSESSMENT

1. What I really like about this piece is _____
   _____
   _____

2. Something new I tried this time is _____
   _____
   _____

3. I had difficulty with _____
   _____
   _____

4. I tried to overcome the difficulty by _____
   _____
   _____

5. Next time I might try and improve on _____
   _____
   _____

You can design a writing record sheet which enables you to record for each piece of writing, your focus for analysis, the student's achievements and future challenges. (See examples in Appendix 8 a,b,c.) For a more detailed analysis of a piece of writing you can use a recording format such as the one shown below.

Writing Analysis Sheet

Name: Title/Topic: _____ Date: _____ Language: _____ _____	
Ideas/Information	Language
Organisation	Mechanics

Constraints of this assessment technique

Analysing students' products and outcomes can provide you with a wealth of information but it is important that this process doesn't occur in isolation from the student whose work is being examined. Students can be actively involved in both establishing the criteria for success and self-analysis of their work (see section "Drawing on student record-keeping and self-assessment" pp.66-76). It is important that your own interpretations about a student's achievements take these into account and that you confirm them through discussion with the student.

Each product needs to be considered not as a separate example, but within the context of everything the student has previously done and all that is known about his/her development to that point. The circumstances in which the work was done and the student's previous experiences of the type of task and attitude to it, are also important considerations when analysing the outcome.

OBSERVING STUDENTS' READING AND WRITING BEHAVIOURS

Analysing products can provide you with a wealth of information about your students' development but there may be gaps in your knowledge of how they operate as readers or writers. You also need to know the *process* students go through to achieve the finished written product, the *strategies* they use as they read and their *attitude* towards different reading and writing tasks. Further information about these can be obtained by observing students as they undertake individual reading and writing tasks or as they work with other students in different group situations.

As you observe students you may pick up incidental information which will tell you about an achievement, a strategy used or an attitude that a student brings to a task. For example as a Junior Primary teacher observed students sharing books she recorded:
> "25/10 James was using the pointer to point to individual words from left to right down the page."

This tells the teacher that James is now able to distinguish individual words and has developed directional knowledge about print.

There may be times when you are observing students with a particular purpose in mind. It could be that you have made an assumption about a student and you want to check it out by observing the student at a particular task. For instance after analysing a student's written product you may notice a lack of organisation and you may think that strategies for planning in the pre-writing stage may be limited. You then observe the student to confirm or deny your prediction. The information can be recorded on a prepared sheet as in the following sample.

Pre-writing strategies

Does the child
• draw
• discuss work with peers
• use classroom resources for ideas
• reflect individually
• look at past writing
• look in books/around room etc:
	Ninh
	
	25/10: Opened folder, look out past work, flipped through sheets found a piece of writing; read it, put it down, sat, picked it up, read: Got out pad, started writing
	
	  * Check out what he wrote
		Michael
		
		26/10: Got folder, back to seat, talked to Chris, opened folder, Shuffled papers, talk to Chris, stare out window. Looked at ideas list in front of folder, talked to Chris, wrote a few lines:
		
		  * Check out conversations — listen in during next observation

Anita 25/10: Drawing on piece of paper. Talk to Melinda, drawing again. 26/10: Writing on drawing from yesterday	Lynley 25/10: Wandering around room. Got a big book, put it on easel. "Thing from Somewhere" Looked at 8 pages, shut it, put it back, back to seat * later — noticed her writing "Monster from Space" story	Brett 26/10: Back to seat with folder: Sat down, took out pad wrote. Read work circled words — wrote

Sometimes observation may be directed by the need to obtain as much information as possible, in a set time, about the whole class. For example you may want to find out the range of books your students are reading. With a class list in hand you can record the books they choose to read during silent reading times over a two week period.

The rest of this section explores the opportunities for observing and the types of information you can obtain, organisational factors and constraints of this assessment technique.

Opportunities for observing reading and writing behaviours
You can observe and record information:
• while students read aloud
• while students read independently
• while students do reading and writing tasks.

Students reading aloud

Listening to students read aloud provides an opportunity for you to find out the kinds of strategies they use as they read. One of the difficulties though is to know what to attend to and how to understand the significance of the things they do and say. Usually when teachers listen to students read they gain a general impression of what they are doing by attending to things like fluency and the expression they use. Whilst these reveal some information about their success on particular books a more specific focus is needed to help teachers to understand the reading strategies students are using and hence their development as readers. The most effective way teachers have of doing this is to record and analyse students' reading behaviours. This can give you insights into:

- the sorts of predications students make
- the basis for the predictions
- the kinds of coping strategies students use as readers
- the nature of the texts students read.

One significant behaviour you can record and analyse is the errors students make when they are reading aloud. Any deviation from the text is considered to be an error. These may be a number of different types, for example:

- a substitution (*house* for *home*, or *watch* for *very*)
- an insertion, the addition of an extra word or words
- an omission, where one or more words is left out.

The important thing about errors is that you can analyse them to see whether the students are reading for meaning, including whether they are making reasonable predictions about how the text will go, and are checking what they have read to ensure that it makes sense. Errors must therefore be analysed in the context of the text and not in isolation.

It is important to monitor whether or not students correct their errors. When students correct their errors it means that they are developing a system for monitoring their own behaviour when reading. It also means that they are making enough sense of the text to realise that they have made an error. The relationship between the number of errors students make and the number of errors they self-correct is an important indicator of their success with a book. If students self-correct nearly all the errors they make then you can usually by satisfied that the book is offering them a successful reading experience. However, if they make inappropriate errors and don't correct them it means that the book is unsuitable for them at this time and they should be given another one on which they can experience success.

Apart from gaining insights into the basic strategies students use and the appropriateness of the books they read, you can also watch for the kinds of strategies they use when they confront a difficulty of some kind. For example you can note behaviours such as:

- finger pointing
- rereading
- repeating words or phrases
- pausing or reading word by word (voice pointing).

Over time you can make an informed decision about whether the student is using appropriately such coping strategies.

If you are interested in using a systematic approach to observing oral reading behaviours you could refer to Clay (1981) where she explains Running Records. This is her system for recording, analysing and understanding young students' oral reading behaviours. Kemp (1987) provides a summary of running record procedures.

If you work with primary age students Goodman and Burke's (1972) *Reading Miscue Inventory* provides for a similar kind of systematic observation and analysis of older students' reading behaviours. A simplified version of a reading miscue inventory, developed in Australia, can be found in Johnson (1979).

Taking Running Records and carrying out the Reading Miscue Inventory may appear daunting at first. Teachers need time to learn to use the notations and special organisational arrangements may be needed so that teachers can work one-to-one with a student. The benefits of learning these techniques, however, are considerable. Once teachers have internalised this way of listening to students reading aloud, they are able to make more informed judgements about students' development as readers. They are also able to identify much more quickly and accurately the students who are at risk as readers.

Students reading independently

There are many classroom occasions when you can spend time observing students reading independently. It could be while they read silently by themselves or when they read in pairs or groups.

During silent reading times you may pursue questions such as:
• do they assume responsibility for choice of reading materials and are they willing to accept or reject books?
• are they able to ignore distractions and stay on task?
• are they choosing to read a range of books?
• do they read books in their home language or English?

While students are sharing books with others you could gather incidental information about them as readers. You may be able to see which students:
• choose to share and discuss books with others
• are able to seek help from their peers or teachers
• are reading with pleasure and satisfaction
• use books for their own purposes
• seek out a bilingual person to read with.

It may be that you observe a group of students reading and discussing a Big Book together during activity time. This gives you the opportunity to focus on their knowledge and understanding of:
• mechanics – letter/sound relationships, punctuation, conventions or devices for showing emphasis

- features of fiction such as settings, outcomes
- features of non-fiction – subheadings, index, contents, instructions.

While students are doing reading and writing tasks

There will be occasions while students are engaged in reading and writing tasks that you will be able to observe and note the strategies they use as readers or writers.

As they are involved in writing you may have a particular question in mind. One way to find out what strategies students are using in the writing stage is to watch them as they write. You may then observe them:
- talking to others about their work
- asking others for help
- rereading work
- referring to notes, plans, diagrams (in home language or in English)
- pausing to think
- consulting word sources around the classroom
- using a bilingual dictionary or resource person
- getting others to proof read
- thinking in their home language and translating into English.

All of these may indicate that the students are aware of some strategies to use for drafting and revising a piece of work.

As you watch the students doing research using non-fiction material it will become more obvious what reading strategies they are using to process the print. You may notice that they are able to:
- skim read
- underline difficult words
- talk with others about the topic
- make an outline or summary
- read material aloud.

All of these behaviours indicate they have coping strategies for making sense of unfamiliar or difficult material.

Watching students undertake tasks that are a response to a book or a story will give you an opportunity to see their creating strategies at work. As they become lost in their play or puppet performance, or in the making of a model or mobile, you will be able to see or note from their responses and interpretations of character how they visualised the setting, the events and the characters that they read about.

Organising for observing reading and writing behaviours
When you include observations as part of your literacy program you will need to:
- provide regular times during the week for this to be used so it becomes part of your normal classroom procedure. Some teachers

find it useful to allocate five minutes of every writing session to observing students' writing behaviours. Similarly, while students are working on reading response activities they set aside regularly ten minutes to hear oral reading.

- consider using a roster so that all students are observed over a set period and time is not wasted deciding on whom to focus. You may find it useful to use a class list and check off at the end of the day/week students on whom you have focused.
- involve the student in the observation, so that they are aware of your purpose. This can be explained to the students at the beginning of the year so that they will then expect it as part of the normal classroom procedure.
- organise an easy and systematic method of recording information . If the documentation to be used is always kept in the same place it will be quickly accessible for use. Examples of observation record sheets are included in Appendix 11 (a,b,c,d). Ways of storing this accumulated information are included in chapter 5, "Storing information".

Constraints of this assessment technique

As you observe students with a particular purpose in mind you will be able to get information that you require. Bear in mind, however that techniques such as Running Records and Miscue Analysis require intense periods of one-to-one observation and further time for analysis. Even during times of incidental observation you will gather a wealth of information that will then need to be interpreted. This interpretation will be done on the basis of your beliefs about literacy development and the significance you see this behaviour as having. It is therefore possible for teachers to interpret behaviours quite differently. For example, a teacher might observe a student looking out of a window during pre-writing. This could be interpreted as time-wasting, or alternatively, that the student is planning what to say.

The interpretation resulting from observation does not stand alone; you need to verify it through talking to the student about what he or she was actually doing.

STUDENT–TEACHER INTERACTIONS

The interpretations you make when you analyse products and outcomes or observe students at work need to be discussed with the students. Talking to students about their learning is a way of confirming the assumptions you have made as a result of other assessment practices, and another very powerful means of gathering information. The individual, small group and whole class situations in which you speak to students are ideal opportunities to find out about aspects of their development.

When you are talking with students who are learning English as a second language, it may be necessary to seek help from ESL teachers, bilingual aides or teachers on the staff. Like language competence, gender is also an important aspect of teacher-student interactions. Research has shown that girls in particular tend to receive less "air-space" and are addressed less often by their teachers. This means making a deliberate effort to provide equal opportunities for each student to talk to you, if you wish this to provide a fair and viable method of collecting information about your students.

The following section explores the classroom opportunities for such interactions and the types of information that can be gathered from them, some organisational factors and the constraints of this technique.

Opportunities for student–teacher interactions
Opportunities for interactions occur:
- during informal conversations
- while students do reading and writing tasks
- during interviews
- during individual conferences
- during group conferences
- during whole class discussions.

Informal conversations

Useful information about a student can be picked up incidentally during an informal chat in the classroom, before or after school, or at break time, for example, a student mentions that she has started keeping a journal, giving her teacher insights into her positive attitude to writing and her concepts about the uses of written language.

While students are doing reading and writing tasks

Discussions will often take place while students are working. Because these interactions are often initiated by students who actually want help with a specific part of the task, they are a useful source of information about the challenges and difficulties the students are encountering. For example, a student who was part way through a first draft of a book review became bogged down in a lengthy description of the plot. From discussion about how to summarise the storyline the teacher found that he:
- made copious notes about the book before beginning to write but didn't go on to identify key points
- had excellent recall of the sequence of events in the story
- was able to blend personal opinion and factual information to give an accurate but persuasive review of the book.

These chats are sometimes referred to as "roving conferences" because they address students' needs in the same way that planned conferences do, but with a narrower and more immediate focus.

Interviews

One direct way to gain specific information about students' reading or writing is to interview them. You will need to have worked out specific questions to get the information you want, e.g. "How do you choose your topics for writing?" Depending on the students' response, further prompting or re-phrasing of the question may be necessary. The following is a set of questions one teacher devised to find out about her students' pre-writing strategies.

> *Have you talked with anyone else about your ideas?*
> *What did they say?*
> *What was your reaction? (verbally and in terms of ideas)*
> *When did you decide on a topic?*
> *How did you decide?*
> *Did you make notes?*
> *If so, when and why?*
> *If not, why not?*
> *Will you use pictures?*
> *Have you drawn any pictures yet?*
> *Why do you want to use pictures?*
> *Why don't you want to use pictures?*
> *Have you collected anything? (e.g. photos, graphs)*
> *How will you write it?*
> *What problems have you encountered?*
> *How did you get over these hurdles?*
> *Are you ready to start writing?*

Obviously the teacher would select which questions are appropriate at any one time.

Individual conferences

As well as talking to students in interviews you can allocate regular times to talk to them about their reading and writing experiences. These discussions are often called conferences. They are used by teachers to respond to what the students are doing at various stages of their writing, or to talk to them about recent reading and the outcomes of this reading. They also provide an excellent opportunity to make assessments of students' achievements and needs.

Writing conferences
In writing conferences with students, the information you can gather will depend on the stage of their writing they are at and which aspects you, or the students, wish to know about. For example, you can focus on:
• the pre-writing strategies they know about and use
• the strategies they use during the drafting and revising phase. The following are the kinds of questions you might ask:
Why did you cross out this section?
Which words will you check for spelling?
What effect were you trying to achieve by rearranging this section?
Have you read any of this to someone else?

- the students' understanding of the ideas, organisation, language and mechanics appropriate to that type of writing (as described in the section on "Analysing students' reading outcomes and writing products", pp.44-53). One advantage of doing this with the students present is that you can ask further clarifying questions. For instance, if you are unclear of the focus of a student's writing you might ask, *What is your main point? Can you tell me what is the most important thing you want to say here?*
- the post-writing options they are aware of
- the difficulties that ESL students are confronting in their writing.

Through reflecting on writing conferences over a period of time it should be possible to add to your understandings of the students' attitudes to particular writing tasks, their growing concepts about literacy and the range of writing experiences they have completed. For example, one teacher noted that a student who had shown a marked preference for factual writing was also developing his awareness of other purposes for writing and had recently written "to amuse".

Reading conferences
Reading conferences can be held for a variety of reasons. Sometimes you can ask students to be prepared to discuss their general reactions to completed reading. At other times you can ask them to focus on a particular aspect of the text by setting a task or questions prior to reading.

The kinds of responses they make in a conference will reveal much about their understandings of the ideas in the text(s) under discussion and also about their awareness of specific aspects of the organisation, language or mechanics of these texts. For example a student who had completed the book *Pippi Longstocking* was asked by her teacher to come to a conference prepared to discuss the main character. In the conference she:
- described her enjoyment of the book
- told about a particularly funny incident
- described the main character as requested.

From these responses the teacher noted that she:
- appreciated the humour of the story
- recognised that it came from the "larger than life" depictions of the main character and her actions
- wanted to read more fiction of the "tall tale" variety.

The teacher then sought more information about her understanding and use of strategies by asking the following questions:
What are some of the differences between the way Pippi lives and the way you live?
Would you like to have a friend like her? Why?
How did you picture the town she lives in?

Group conferences

You can also find out about your students' development by talking to them in small group conferences about their reading and writing. These conferences give them the chance to share ideas and responses with each other, while providing you with an opportunity to monitor their interaction to see what it reveals about them as readers and writers. Group conferences can provide the following focuses.

Sharing and responding to each other's writing
For this focus you may need to show students the types of responses that will give the writers information about the effects of their writing on readers. Once students begin to respond in these ways, you will be able to analyse their responses and the writers' replies for what they show about their knowledge of the ideas, organisation, language and mechanics of that type of writing. For example the student who asks the writer of a mystery story, "Why did the woman steal the diamonds?" is showing awareness that motive is an important feature of a mystery story. The writer's response to this question should indicate whether the student also recognises that including this detail will make the crime more believable.

Aspects of the writing process
For instance, the students may share the pre-writing strategies they use and compile a combined list for future reference. Through listening to their contributions and eliciting more information through questioning you can find out information about the strategies each student uses. Similarly discussions about the types of writing the students enjoy or find difficult, or about the purposes for writing, will tell you about their attitudes to particular writing tasks and their concepts about the uses of writing.

Discussing reading and sharing reading outcomes
Once again, you will probably need to demonstrate to students the kinds of questions they can ask each other that will help them as readers to think about their reaction to the texts and their understandings of what they have read. Some teachers provide students with examples of focus questions (see example in Appendix 6.) From observing how the students behave in these conferences you will be able to gain information about their attitudes to particular books and tasks, the strategies they've used to make sense of their reading, and their comprehension of the ideas, organisation, language and mechanics of the text.

Developing students' reading strategies
For instance you may introduce the group to a technique such as reciprocal teaching which will develop their strategies for coping with difficult text. This reciprocal teaching procedure shows students how to go through the steps of:
• reading a paragraph
• asking questions related to the content

- summarising its content
- clarifying difficult words and any confusions
- making predictions about what will come next.

The way each student performs these steps will give you insights into the coping strategies that they can draw on to carry out this task and you may also get a better understanding of the strategies they need to learn.

Whole class discussions

There will be times when you have whole class discussions, meetings or sharing times in which the focus is on a particular aspect of reading or writing. Although you may see these primarily as teaching situations, they can also be used to find out information about each student's literacy development.

You can organise a regular *Circle Time* in which each student has a chance to tell about a favourite book or state an opinion about some aspect of the class novel. From listening to these contributions you can gather information about each student's attitude to reading, preferences for various types of material, and understandings about parts of a particular text.

Whole class sessions can also be used for students sharing and responding to each other's writing. One teacher has a regular time each morning when her year 1/2 students can read their writing aloud. She encourages audience response in the form of questions such as the following list:

> *Why did you write this?*
> *Who did you write for?*
> *What type of writing is it?*
> *Where did you get your ideas from?*
> *What has helped you when writing?*
> *What will you do with this writing?*
> *How do you feel about this writing?*

From the writer's answers she finds out about their concepts about literacy, attitudes and strategies.

Organising to talk to students

Although talking to students is a natural part of teaching, it is necessary to organise for it to occur in ways that enhance learning and provide for systematic assessment. Here are some ways to do this.

Time allocation

Allocate time for individual and group conferences and whole class sharing to occur. For instance, students can be rostered for individual conferences at set times over a fortnight, or you can allow time each day for conferences as students need them and tick students off on a class list to ensure you see each of them during a fortnight . Group conferences can also be rostered, or organised on the basis of need. For example, you might call together all the students who would like to talk about their writing at the beginning of a writing session. Or students may know that if they go and sit in a designated palce during writing time they will be joined by other students who are prepared to give them a response to their writing.

Whole class sharing sessions
These can be built into your ongoing program. Many teachers find it useful to begin reading or writing sessions with this type of sharing.

Preparation
Ensure students know what to expect from each type of interaction so that they can prepare for it and can have some control over what they get out of it. This might mean that when students come to a writing conference to discuss a completed draft they need to have already made notes of the aspects they would like to talk about. Some teachers provide students with written guidelines to assist them to prepare for individual or group conferences.

Conference Writing Record

Name...
Date...

                                              Non-fiction ☐

I need a conference about my writng. It is a   Fiction ☐
.... about ....

I have read my writing to see if it makes sense. ☐

I have used ∧ to put in missed out words. ☐

I have neatly crossed out words not needed. ☐

I have put capital letters at the beginning of sentences and for names. ☐

I have put full stops at the end of sentences. ☐

I have neatly underlined the spelling I need to check. ☐

I have checked the spelling with -

     my folder ☐
     a dictionary ☐
     wall chart ☐
     a friend ☐
     .... ☐

I shared my writing with my friend ....

My friend helped me to see if it made sense. ☐

My friend helped me with my spelling. ☐

My friend said the best part was ....

My friend wanted to know more about ....
....

I am ready for a conference ☐

(See Reading example in Appendix 9.)

Development of interaction skills
Plan to develop students' personal interaction skills so that participation in group situations is equitable, with each student being able to contribute openly without fear of "put-downs." Many teachers spend the first few weeks of the year concentrating on activities that develop students' ability to work in groups and then continue to emphasise these skills throughout the year.

Recording of interactions
Work out efficient ways for you and the students to record the most important aspects of your interactions. It may mean organising an easily accessible system for jotting down anecdotal notes, such as a card file or a notebook. When you notice something significant while talking to a student it can be quickly noted either immediately or when you have a moment. Some teachers have a special record sheet for noting students' development in reading and writing (see example in Appendix 9).

The students may have a special section of a "Record Book" (see chapter 5, "Storing information", pp.83-88) in which to record their own discussion points for conferences, as well as key points arising from the conferences.

Date	Title	Things I Need to Discuss	Conference Discussion Points

Constraints of this assessment technique
Talking to students as an assessment technique can have limitations if efforts are not made to ensure that all students have equal access to this procedure. You will have found that there are individual differences in the degree to which students will voluntarily interact with you and each other. These differences may be due to students' varying dispositions, cultural backgrounds or gender expectations.

The amount of useful information gained can also be limited by the type of questions you ask. Closed questions that require minimal response, or questions that pre-empt the student's own reflections, will not yield very much information about the student's reading or writing development. Questions need to be carefully considered and framed in ways that get the information you require. Because of the difficulty of thinking of good questions on the spot, some teachers find it useful to devise lists of focus questions for both their own and their students' use in discussing reading and writing experiences. (See examples in Appendix 6 & 7.)

Finding uninterrupted time to talk to students in individual and group conferences often proves a big stumbling block for teachers. It requires organising your teaching program so that students are able to work independently leaving you free to work with individuals or groups. This can mean spending considerable time teaching students the routines for independent work, especially if they are used to being teacher dependent. With a new class it can take quite a few weeks to establish the atmosphere of trust and cooperation that is necessary if students are to feel comfortable enough to talk to you and each other openly.

DRAWING ON STUDENT RECORD-KEEPING AND SELF-ASSESSMENT

As well as talking with students, you may like to consider how students' regular written reflections on their learning might provide you with information. Viewed over time and across a range of reading and writing tasks, written reflections can allow you valuable insights into the way your students operate, how they view themselves as learners, what they understand about literacy and what help they might need. Where students are too inexperienced to write or have a disability, teachers can obtain information through talking or through having students record their ideas by other means such as drawing or ticking boxes.

The following section explores some opportunities for student recording and self-assessment and the types of information that can be gathered, some organisational factors and the constraints of this technique.

Opportunities for student record-keeping and self- assessment

Some opportunities for student self-evaluative and record-keeping activities can be created by requiring students to:
- keep records of reading and writing
- record interests and background data
- reflect on themselves as readers and writers
- reflect on recent tasks
- comment on written products
- devise and negotiate guidelines or criteria for success.

The age, year level and experience of your students will determine the degree to which these activities can be carried out and the support they will need from you.

Keeping records of reading and writing

Students can carry out much of the routine record-keeping for reading and writing assessment. Analysing these records can provide you with the following types of information:
- kinds of reading and writing in which students are engaged
- frequency with which they choose particular material for reading (in English and in their home language)

- quantity of material/books read over a particular period
- books left unfinished
- source of reading material (home, school library, friend, etc.)
- frequency with which they write in particular genres or forms
- various purposes they have for writing or reading
- number and kinds of writing taken through to publishing
- number and kinds of writing left unfinished
- variety of publishing forms chosen.

The following is an example of how students in a year 4 classroom keep a reading record.

MY READING RECORD

Title Author/Call no.	Oral Rdg. 2 pages Read to Signed	Discussed Book with Signed	Conference with teacher Date Signed	Activity Completed Signed	Genre	Rating 9-10 Excellent 7-8 Good 5-6 O.K. 1-4 awful	Purpose
Gymnastics Author: Brian Hayhurst Call no. 796.4 HAY	Read to: Meagan Signed: Meagan	Discussed book with Meg Signed: Meagan	20/10	Book report	non-fiction	1-8	Joy
Its Not the end of the world, Call No. Fblu	Read to: Gemma Signed: Gemma	Discussed with Gemma Signed: Gemm	27/10	Book Jacket	fiction novel	1-8	Joy
Taggie's House Call No. Fblu	Read to: Sharon Signed:	Discussed with Sharon Signed:	3/11	Book review	novel	1-8	intrested
Making Presents	Read to: Ila Signed:	Discussed with: signed: Ila		10 Word Description	non-fiction	1-8	to make things
Blubber Call No. Fblu Judy Blume	Read to: signed:	Discussed with: signed:		1 Illustration	novel	1-8	Title
Roberts A Pilot	Read to: Gemma signed: Gem.	Discussed with Gem Signed: Gemma		Front cover	Picture	1-8	Just to read
James and The giant Peach Roald Dahl	Read to: Gem signed: Gemma	Discussed With Gem Signed: Gemma		4 Illustrations	Novel	9	Because of author
More Brain Ticklers	Read to: Sharon Signed Sharon	Discussed with Sharon Signed: Sharon			non-fiction		I was in a rush
Freckle Juice	Read to: Sharon Signed: Sharon	Discussed With: Sharon Signed: Sharon					

Recording interests and background data

In our multicultural society, knowing about the backgrounds of your students is essential to your understanding of them as learners because it enables you to:

- acknowledge and value cultural differences, bilingualism and Aboriginality
- understand how students learn English as a second language
- understand different values and attitudes
- understand the trauma of migration.

One way to get access to this information is to involve your students in a Survey of Family Origins. Students can be asked to take home a brief questionnaire and interview their parents to discover where their ancestors came from.

Interest Inventories are another kind of questionnaire which you might use at the beginning of the year, as a class "getting-to-know-each-other" exercise. Interest Inventories can provide information about students':
- home reading and writing habits
- likes and dislikes
- sports, clubs, hobbies, interests
- cultural and family backgrounds
- the extent and range of students' reading and writing activities at home compared to other pastimes, such as television viewing.

They may also reveal gender-based attitudes and concepts about the value and status of literacy activities, as well as cultural influences on students' learning.

An example of an Interest Inventory is contained in Appendix 12.

Reflecting on themselves as readers and writers

Analysing students' written perceptions of themselves as readers and writers is another way of obtaining valuable information, particularly at the beginning of a year when you are trying to find out as much about your new students as you can. You may find out about students' abilities to review their past performances, their perceived strengths, needs and current challenges, and their ability or willingness to make some definite plans or resolutions for improving. The task can be repeated around the middle of the year, when students can be invited to reflect on what they originally wrote about themselves, and decide whether or not they have achieved their aims, and what they might do in order to continue to develop. This again will provide you with valuable insights into students' perceptions of their efforts and achievements.

Two variations of this task are described below. Each will result in slightly different kinds of information from your students.

One variation is to ask your students to reflect on themselves as readers and writers. You will need to provide some guidelines, which students can use to assist their thinking. For example:

Me As A Reader

What do you think about yourself as a reader?
What kinds of books do you enjoy? Why?
What kinds of books do you find difficult? Why?
What challenges in reading could you set yourself this year?
What help will you need to achieve them?
What will you need to do yourself to achieve them?

Here is an example from a year 5 student:

Me as a Reader.

I like reading mistrey books. and books that aren't that long and I like reading B.F.G. because it is funny. and I like reading Boss of the pool. I think I am getting better at reading. best of all I like reading Robin Klein books. and I like reading nearly all day. When I am older I would like to be a writer. So I can write alot of storys for children I like reading comcies. one of my favrote is mad BOOKS. they are good. I like reading the neius paper. and Magazins. I like reading smash hits. on the Bus. and singing all the songs in their. I like reading soft covered Books.

A second variation is to provide students with a prepared sheet containing questions for them to answer as in this example from a year 2 classroom:

Name . . . . Date . . . .

Draw a picture of yourself doing your best writing.

List some things that help to make writing easy for you.

when you are with a friend . . . .
when you are by yourself . . . when you are at home .
when it is quit. . . . .

What can sometimes make writing hard?

when it is noisy . . . .
when your freend keeps talking to you . . . .

. . . .

What is your best thing you have written so far this year?

My story about the Magic wish . . . .

. . . . Was it published? yes . . . .

What was really good about this writing?

The Picures are good . . . .
it was typed . . . .
I Drew the Pictures . . . .

Both of these tasks allow students to have some input into your programming. By taking their answers seriously and where possible making adjustments in accordance with their comments you can demonstrate that you are sincere in wanting to help them to achieve success. In a sense you are inviting students to:

• take some responsibility for setting up the optimum conditions for their success
• have a say in the organisation of the classroom for writing and reading
• have more of an investment in making sure it works.

Students' writing in response to the first task – *Me As a Reader* – will be in prose form, and because of the relatively flexible nature of the task, you may find that students are more likely to write extended comments and to elaborate on their thoughts to make their meanings clear. This is probably a more challenging task than the second option. In questionnaires like the one described in the second task, students characteristically tend to write short, direct answers, almost in list form, and seem to need less mental energy to complete the task. The way you design the task will affect the type of information you will receive, and you will need to design the task according to the kind of information you require. Appendix 13 is another example of a *Me as a Writer* sheet.

Reflecting on recent tasks

Writing or talking about their learning in recent tasks enables students to reflect and provide you with information on such things as:

• their understanding of the nature and purpose of the task
• their enjoyment of and engagement with the task
• the usefulness of the models and other help you provided
• the amount and kind of help they got from peers, parents, AEW, bilingual aide, others
• the most challenging aspects of the task
• the most significant things they learnt from the task
• their ideas for improvement the next time they tackle a similar task.

Providing focus questions or guidelines helps students to stay on the topic and think about relevant aspects of the task. Regularly using the same format sets students up for success by letting them in on what you think is important and giving them a structure for thinking about their learning. For example, you may require students to spend some time each Friday reviewing the past week's work. It could be helpful to provide students with a list of questions to guide their reflections:

Weekly Review
What do you feel you have learnt/achieved this week?
What activities did you find interesting or useful?
In what areas do you feel you need more help?
What areas do you feel you need more practice with?
What are your plans or intentions for next week in regard to any of the above?

It is important to respond to students' written evaluations in writing yourself. This will provide you with an ideal opportunity to demonstrate that you take their comments seriously and that you value their self-appraisals, suggestions and ideas. Your responses can assist students to become more accurate and thoughtful in their reflections, by:

• signalling your agreement with particular comments
• offering suggestions
• responding to requests for help as soon as possible
• referring them to other sources of information
• demonstrating the types of comments they might make
• congratulating them on astute evaluations
• commiserating with them about disappointments they mention
• specifically mentioning students' achievements which you've noticed.

Below is an example of a year 4 student's weekly review and the teacher's response:

TO   14th

This week it has been good at school for math it is getting better because I am not afraied to put my hand up. can we plese do art more because we havent been having art verry ofen. story wrighting is getting better because you have put that Tittle thing up. I can get more stoyes up and Iders know the titles are up. I know this sounds stupid But some times when I cant think of a story to wright I say can I do a story with some one

                        from
                        xxxxxxx
                        ooooooo

Dear .
        I'm glad you're putting your hand up when you aren't sure about something. I've noticed that lots of your questions are very good ones.
        We didn't have art this week because it was a short week with Monday being a holiday and we had too much else to fit in.
        I'm glad the titles sheet is helping your story writing and, you know, it doesn't sound at all silly to ask to write a story with someone else when you can't think of something to write on your own. Lots of people do that, even adults (especially adults!) Another thing you can do is ask someone else to help you get started, perhaps just to talk about a few ideas for 5 minutes and then you can both write your own stories.
        Have a good week,

Throughout the year the weekly review can be maintained, but from time to time you might want the students to engage in more specific reflection related to particular literacy themes or units of work which are a current feature of your program. For example, if you have spent some time demonstrating, discussing and having students engage in getting information from reference books, you might want them to reflect on their efforts in this area . You could add a general question to the weekly review, e.g. "This week I would like you to tell me what you did when you were gathering your information for your Animal Project". Another option is to prepare a sheet of more specific questions, as in the following example:

Topic *Animal projet*

Name   **Date**

What was the best thing about this topic?

For Finding out and going to the library to do research.

What were the most important things that you learnt during this topic? or Are there any new things that you can now do?

Mostly how to set projects out. Draw a bit better. I learnt about 20 new things about bears. It was exciting and my fist individual project

Was there anything that you found difficult to do? What?

Yes, drawing things that looked like they were alive, also trying to make the background like the animals habitat.

How do you feel about this topic? Circle the words that best describe your feelings. (Interested, successful, confused, bored, worried, clever, excited, fascinated.)

Is there anything that you want to know about the topic now? (Or anything extra that you'd like to do?)

Yes of course. I'd like to know how the bears babies are going + going Like they could try and send me a weekly report

Give your opinion of your work in this theme. (Did you achieve your goals, your use of time, your research – was it successful? etc.) What will you do differently next time?

Yes I achevied + achived my goals and I'm happy only about that but I wasted a lot of time

---

Analysing their own writing

Students can be encouraged to reflect on their achievements with a particular piece of writing. In the following example, Nick wrote about "Our New Motor," and then told what he thought was good about the particular piece of writing.

OUR New moToR.

nine Weeks ago my DaD brought a
New moTor. IT Jis a Jv8 moTor. he had
Washed iT down with petrol. And now
The Shed smells. lasT nionT my baby
SiTer Was helping me fill The wood BOX
AND The coloenT come in The sheD
Becaus She han a smoke AND Dad
PuT The motor in our car. yesTerDay
He spray panted Some Things.

8 SepT.
Our new moTor
I Think iT is goon Beacause I useD
Some worDs. ThaT harcley ever Be newseD.
AnD I puT a BiT of show noT Tell.

Nick's teacher subsequently congratulated him on his effort and
pointed out to him that his comments showed his awareness of the
importance of using interesting language. In future writings, Nick
might be encouraged to follow up this emphasis on language, or to
reflect on other aspects of written products:

• the ideas he used
• the organisation of his piece of writing
• the mechanics, such as spelling or punctuation.

You might also want to ask students to evaluate the writing strategies
they used during a particular writing task.

Thinking About My Writing

Name_____ Date_____

Title My exCiTing News Form STORY

1. Before writing I... ThoughT aBouT my aunTies
weDDing

2. During writing I... ThoughT aBouT PuTting
in my sTory ThaT I
have To look afTer Two
2 year olDs

3. After writing I... goT exciTeD aBouT/T

4. If you could write this again what would you do
differently? PuT ThaT The liTTle
ones will Be Wearing
The same Dress as me

5. What did you learn when doing this writing?
ThaT weDDings
are specIAl

6. How do you feel about this writing? (um?)
goon Because I ThoughT
aBouT my aunTie

Devising and negotiating their own guidelines or criteria for success

As students become more experienced in evaluating their performance, they can begin to take a major role in deciding on their own criteria for success. This can be done during small group sessions, where students pool their collective wisdom and devise lists which can be used as guidelines for everyone in the group. For example, if you want students to become more aware of the various editing skills they need to use, you might ask the class to work in groups to devise lists of all the editing issues they can think of. Students working on the following task in a year 5 classroom recently included these statements:

Language conventions

1   Put a full. stop at the end of a sentence (.)

2   Put a capital at the start of a sentence or a Name (L)

3   Put speech marks when some one talks (" ")

4. Put a question mark after a question (?)

5. if there is two meanings put Brackets around one ( )

6   put a Exlamation mark if some body talks loud(!)

7. When you talk about some thing diffrent Do a paragraph

8. Commers are insted of writing and. (Beverly, Louisa, craig and Jason)

9. this is a sentence (I am sick.)

10. a collen is when you are going to say the same thing but in diffrent words

11.

The list was discussed, revised, put into priority order, and eventually transformed into an editing checklist, to be kept by each student for reference when editing a piece of writing.

EDITING CHECKLIST

Name:										
Full stops at end of sentence.										
Capital letter – beginning of sentence name of person or place.										
Comma – pause but don't stop. List of things.										
Question mark – end of a question.										
Speech marks – beginning and end of speech. **Start new line when someone speaks. Start new line after someone speaks.**										
Exclamation mark – to show surprise. For loudness. For humorous effect.										
New paragraph – When you begin to write about something slightly different. Start new paragraph about 5 spaces in from the margin.										
Apostrophe – To show ownership (Jeff's book). To show a letter is missing (isn't).										

Organising for students' record-keeping and self-assessment

If you want to include student self-evaluation in your literacy program, you will need to provide a great deal of support particularly during the introductory period, in the following ways:

- show students how you reflect on your own writing during think-aloud writing demonstrations
- encourage students to evaluate their efforts in discussions during reading and writing conferences with individuals
- provide time for students to learn from each other by sharing their reflections in pairs, small groups and whole class discussions
- show your students some written evaluations which have been done by other students. If you think students may be sensitive about sharing their self-evaluations with others, borrow some anonymous examples from other teachers, or use some of the examples from this book. Start saving a collection now for showing to future classes!
- provide regular times for individual written reflections–perhaps at the end of the day, once or twice a week. Let students know that these times will be part of the normal program, so that they can get into the habit of preparing for them
- make time to write back to your students and respond to their comments
- organise to check students' perceptions of themselves with parents and others to ensure you get a balanced view.

Constraints of this assessment technique

The extent of junior primary children's record-keeping and written evaluations may be limited, but many teachers have found ways of designing tasks which overcome this obstacle. Below is an example of how junior primary students can record the different types of writing they do. The student has marked with a star the kinds of writing he has completed during the term.

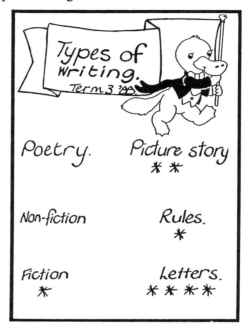

The value of student self-evaluation will be less if the activity is over-used, or if the routines become too complex or too tedious. You will need to monitor students' replies and reactions closely, respond to them promptly, and ensure that the importance of self-evaluation in learning is understood. Questionnaires with too many questions may overtax the attention span of some students, so that their replies are ill-considered and the information you receive misleading.

COLLECTING INFORMATION FROM PARENTS, CARE-GIVERS AND OTHERS

So far the assessment techniques described have been those that are used in classrooms. However, as partners with you in their children's education, parents and caregivers can offer you vital information about their children's learning and development. Colleagues who also work with your students can also offer useful information about them. Both groups can provide you with information which may reinforce or challenge your own assessment of a student's development.

The rest of this section explores some opportunities for collection and the type of information you can obtain, organisational factors and constraints of this assessment technique. In particular, teachers need to be sensitive to all living arrangements of their students — not all children live in a nuclear family setting. The learning needs of children living in substitute care will be enhanced through close communication with caregivers.

Opportunities for collecting information from parents, caregivers and others
Information may be obtained through:
- talking with parents at school and, where appropriate, during home visits
- written information from parents and caregivers
- reviewing past records and reports
- talking with colleagues.

Talking with parents and caregivers

There are many opportunities for you to talk with parents and caregivers as part of your normal classroom program. At set times throughout the year you may organise to have interviews with these people. These interviews may be at your request or theirs. They may be for you to:
- become acquainted with parents and caregivers
- discuss the student's progress
- discuss a problem concerning the student.

If you have Aboriginal children in your classroom you should discuss with your school's Aboriginal Resource Teacher ways in which you may work with Aboriginal parents in their children's learning.

While talking with parents and caregivers you can find out:
- how their children use literacy outside the school environment
- the parents' and caregivers' perceptions of their children as readers and writers
- the challenges that they see their child has faced and overcome
- their view of their children's progress and the influences they think may be contributing to success or failures.

To improve the effectiveness of interviews it is necessary to ensure that parents and caregivers are aware of your purpose for speaking with them prior to the interviews. For instance, your purpose may be to:
- exchange information about the student's progress
- discuss a particular problem
- highlight achievements
- discuss plans for helping students' literacy development.

Again ask your Aboriginal Resource Teacher to assist you with ideas for working together with Aborginal parents and caregivers.

One way to let these people know your purpose for interviews is to send a questionnaire to them before the interview so that they have had time to reflect on the questions and talk with their children. For instance if your intention is to exchange information about the student's progress the questions you ask may include:

What have you seen as your child's strengths?

What difficulties do you think your child has faced?

What challenges do you think your child has had this term?

Are there any other issues/concerns that you would like to discuss at the interview?

These replies will give you an indication of parents' and caregivers' concerns and their perceptions of their children's learning. This will help you focus on mutual concerns/issues at the ensuing interview.

To be effective with NESB parents you may need to use the services of a translator for verbal and /or written communication.

Analysing written information from parents and caregivers

There are a variety of techniques for providing parents and caregivers with opportunities for giving you written information about their children. However, it is important to be sensitive to the possibility that some of your students' parents/caregivers may not be literate in English or that some may not yet understand our education system clearly enough to recognise the purpose of your requesting written information about their child from them. It is important therefore that teachers acknowledge the need to develop an agreed way of working with individual parents and caregivers.

To illustrate how written information from parents and caregivers can enhance your understanding of each child consider one technique some junior primary teachers use to learn about students' reading at home. A Reading Memo Book is kept in a cover, folder or plastic bag with the current book the student is reading. There is an exchange of information from parent/caregiver to teacher about the former's insights into the students' oral reading behaviours away from the school setting. For example, Rebecca's mum's comments followed an earlier discussion with the teacher about not forcing the issue of reading:

"Good work. Rebecca doesn't lose her temper now when she is stuck on a word and she tries working it out. She's really improving."

This showed the teacher that the parent had relaxed more while hearing reading and Rebecca had responded. Alternatively a Reading Memo Book may be used to check out an assumption that the teacher has made of particular students. The writing from Lucy's dad about Lucy's reading of *Just Awful*

"Lucy can concentrate better when she is home. Gets distracted easily. She did a good job reading this one."

This was a confirmation for the teacher that the difficulties Lucy was experiencing in concentrating at school were also seen in the home setting.

CHILD'S NAME ....

DATE OF BIRTH ....

CURRENT TERM AT SCHOOL ....

1. What impresses you about your child? (strengths)

   Helpfulness in the home, developing sense of humour
   Interest in what Dad does & his questioning ability.

2. In what ways do you share reading with your child?

   Sam reads his reader to us every weeknight & then
   we read a story to him, most nights.

3. List your child's interests.

   Bikes, anything Dad does, tractors, writing.

4. Any particular favourties in:
   music tapes - Peter Coombe - "toffee apple"
   books - "Shy the platypus," tractor books & generally all books
   authors -
   illustrators -
   nursery rhymes -

5. Tick the activites which your child enjoys:

✓	Choosing books to read	✓	Visiting library
✓	Drawing	✓	Shopping
✓	Writing	✓	Going to newsagency
	Singing	✓	Watching television
✓	Outdoor activities		Computer Games
✓	Talking with others	✓	Helping Mum/Dad
✓	Playing with friends	✓	Being read to
✓	Construction activities		Any other? Collecting chook eggs

6. What areas would you like me to expand on at the Information evening?

   Is the alphabet as I know it, being taught or is this
   unecessary? How to go about reading the reader with the
   child at home? Are my excpectations of my childs
   reading ability high?

Another way to get quite specific information is by sending home questionnaires for parents and caregivers to fill in. These may cover a range of information such as the students' attitudes to reading and writing, parents' perceptions of their child's strengths and weaknesses or uses of literacy at home.

In the example above a teacher sent the questionnaire to parents prior to an information evening.

Reviewing past records and reports

Past reports and records can be used to check out a development or concern. It may be that you want to see if the difficulties the student is having were indicated in previous work. You could be concerned over the fact that the student is reluctant to accept challenges. You could review the past records to see if this is a new development or has been recorded previously.

Talking with colleagues

On occasion you may need to talk with colleagues regarding their perceptions of the students as readers and writers. Librarians are in an ideal position to give you information about the range of books that the students borrow and their attitude towards reading while in the library.

If students in your class work with Special Education teachers, Aboriginal Education Workers, Languages other than English (LOTE) or English as a Second Language (ESL) teachers, or other subject specialist teachers, you may get information from them about their perceptions of the students' literacy backgrounds, strengths, challenges and tasks that they face while working with them.

Organising for collecting information from parents, caregivers and others

If you want information from parents, caregivers and others you will need to consider:
- the time at which an interview can take place without interruptions
- the time and thought needed for effectively designing and analysing your questionnaire
- the help you will need from translators in the preparation and analysis of questionnaires and the time needed for this process
- the occasions when the questionnaires will be sent and how this will be done
- the method of storing and recording information obtained. (See chapter 5, "Storing information", pp.83-88.)

Constraints of this assessment technique

The amount and quality of the information obtained from this method will depend on:
- the relationship that you have with parents and caregivers and the degree that they trust you
- the type and tone of questions you ask
- your response to what they tell you
- whether or not parents, and caregivers see it as an intrusion into their privacy
- parents' and caregivers' own literacy and language skills in English or in their home language.

The next chapter suggests some practical ways of making the related documentation of the assessment techniques described in this chapter manageable, retrievable and time effective.

COLLECTING INFORMATION : OVERVIEW

TECHNIQUE	INFORMATION OBTAINED	OPPORTUNITIES FOR USE
Administering tests	• Aspects of comprehension • Aspects of written products • Strategies used in reading	• Using published tests, writing • Using published tests, reading • Using teacher made tests
Analysing students' reading outcomes and writing products	• Concepts about literacy • Attitudes to reading and writing • Aspects of written products • Aspects of reading comprehension • Strategies for reading and writing • Range of reading and writing forms and purposes	• While students are doing reading and writing tasks • During reading and writing conferences • Collecting samples of students' work
Observing students' reading and writing behaviours	• Attitudes to reading and writing • Aspects of reading comprehension • Strategies for reading and writing • Range of reading and writing forms and purposes	While students are: • reading aloud • reading independently • doing reading and writing tasks
Student-teacher interactions	• Concepts about literacy • Attitudes to reading and writing • Aspects of written products • Aspects of comprehension • Strategies used in reading/writing • Rangeof reading and writing forms and purposes	• Informal conversations • While students doing reading, writing tasks • Interviews • Individual conferences • Group conferences • Whole class discussions
Drawing on student record keeping and self-assessment	• Concepts about literacy • Attitudes to reading and writing • Aspects of written products • Aspects of reading comprehension • Strategies for reading and writing • Range of reading and writing forms and purposes	Students: • keeping records of their reading and writing • recording their interests and back ground data about themselves • reflecting on themselves as readers and writers • reflecting on recent tasks • analysing their own written products • devising and negotiating their own guidelines or criteria for success
Collecting information from parents, caregivers and others	• Concepts about literacy • Attitudes to reading and writing • Strategies for reading and writing • Range of reading and writing forms and purposes	• Talking with parents and caregivers • Analysing written information from parents and caregivers • Reviewing past records and reports • Talking with colleagues

5   STORING INFORMATION

A manageable assessment system provides access to information
from a variety of sources, and organises the collection and storage of
information as simply as possible. If you provide for a variety of
alternative sources of information, your system can survive the
inevitable breakdown in collection which occurs in any classroom
from time to time. An advantage of keeping the data-gathering
simple, predictable and uncomplicated is that your students will be
able to take on much of the record-keeping themselves.

This chapter describes some options for storing information. There is
a degree of overlap between them, as some items could feasibly be
stored in any of two or three different locations. The combinations of
options you choose will be influenced by your decisions about what
information you really need to have access to, what you must record
yourself, what the students can record and what should be shared with
parents and caregivers.

Options for storing information discussed here are:
- writing folder or book
- reading folder or book
- spelling book
- student's record book
- student's assessment folder or file
- communication folder
- teacher's assessment file.

WRITING FOLDER OR BOOK
Students' writing folders can be made from folded cardboard or
adapted from manilla folders. Some teachers prefer to use a writing
book, to avoid the problem of loose pages getting lost. These folders
or books have a dual purpose: to hold writing that students are
currently working on and to contain writing guidelines and assessment
information, such as:
- lists of achievements and challenges
- record of range of writing tasks attempted and works published

- lists of high frequency words to aid spelling
- editing checklist
- topic lists
- conference notes
- personal spelling list, e.g. words from *Have-a-go* sheet.

READING FOLDER OR BOOK
This may be in the form of a cardboard cover or small notebook and contain such things as:
- dated records of books read
- reading conference notes
- comments from parent about home reading
- student's written responses to books read.

SPELLING BOOK
The purpose of a spelling book is to help provide students with a systematic way of developing spelling proficiency. It therefore also provides assessment information about:
- spelling attempts, approximations - invented spelling
- types of spelling errors
- spelling patterns which need attention, e.g. "ea" words
- words now spelt correctly.

STUDENT'S RECORD BOOK
One effective way of making the recording of assessment information manageable for students is to provide them with a book especially for this purpose. The student's record book can be a 96-page exercise book or similar, divided into sections. When introducing the idea to students, you should probably limit the number of sections, e.g:
- Student self-assessments
- Conference notes
- Range of reading and writing
- Lists of achievements and challenges.

Self-assessments

This first section of the book would probably need the most pages allocated to it. Here students write their regular reviews and self-assessments and you write your responses. It could also contain reflective writing, e.g. the *Me as a Writer* task described in the previous chapter.

Conference notes

This second section could begin about three quarters of the way through the book. Students could use it to note what they want to discuss when preparing for a conference. During the actual conference they could record any useful comments made to them by teacher, peers or AEWs, bilingual aides and others. You could also use this section to jot down anything you want the student to remember.

Range of reading and range of writing

Perhaps a double page or more could be allocated at the back of the book to record each reading and writing activity that students do.

Later additions

Once the students become familiar with using this record book you could add other items, such as an editing checklist, or conference questions guidelines. The following example is what a student's record book might look like.

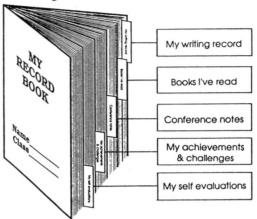

Modifications for various year levels

Some middle primary teachers use a version of this idea called *My Reflection Book*. They have included sections such as a daily review. Students use this section in the last ten minutes of each day to reflect on activities and record tasks they particularly enjoyed, things they need to spend more time on the following day and areas where they need help.

Junior Primary teachers have designed a version called an *About Me* book to allow younger students to use the book according to their particular needs, abilities and interests. Students use this book for such purposes as writing or drawing their self-evaluations and goals, recording their temporary spellings and pasting in special work.

For students to use this book effectively, you may need to guide them fairly closely through the initial setting-out stage, in a step-by-step manner. Demonstrate labelling the different sections, ruling up the pages, putting in the appropriate headings. Careful training sessions in the early stages will result in your students soon being able to use the book competently and effectively.

STUDENT'S ASSESSMENT FOLDER OR FILE
This folder or file can be used to hold the following kinds of assessment information:
- selected samples of written products with teacher's analysis or comments attached
- reading miscue analysis or running record sheets
- anecdotal notes (if in loose-leaf form)
- interest inventories
- student questionnaires
- cumulative list of student achievements/challenges
- computer disks or printouts

- student's self-evaluative letters to teacher
- samples of work selected by student, with comments by teacher and/or student.

COMMUNICATION FOLDER

While personal contact and discussion is the most desirable form of contact with parents and caregivers, a communication folder is one way of setting up a regular, supplementary two-way communication. Material which might be sent home at regular intervals in this folder could include:
- information about the teacher's expectations
- information about the class program
- selected samples of written products
- selected samples of student's self-evaluation
- letters to parents/caregivers from student or teacher about student's achievements or goals
- parent/caregivers' responses
- parent/caregiver surveys
- class newsletters
- samples of work selected by student, with comments by teacher and student.

Your personal contact with parents and caregivers will guide your action in relation to the appropriateness of particular strategies.

TEACHER'S ASSESSMENT FILE

The specific record keeping which you need to do will probably consist of two kinds: anecdotal notes, and cumulative records of each student's learning.

Anecdotal notes can be stored in the student's assessment folder, or pasted into the individual student's record book, if you want to share the information with the student. Other information can be recorded in a separate teacher's book, or perhaps a section of your programming book.

Cumulative records about students' literacy development using the CAASR framework strategies can be kept in a variety of ways. You might devise a system of cards, a book or a folder with separate pages for each student, where dated written comments about significant learning can be recorded. The CAASR framework can be used to devise a "reminder list" of possible aspects on which to comment. This list could be pasted in the front of your record or programming book for easy reference when recording information about individual students. Appendix 14(a) is an example of a reminder list for writing, used by a middle primary teacher. Alternatively, you may prefer to photocopy checklists on separate sheets for each student.

In the following example a year 3 teacher has devised a checklist for easy reference when recording information about a student's reading progress.

NAME: –

ATTITUDES/INTERESTS

* attitude to reading
* reading interests
* favourite books
* borrows from library
* self selects appropriately
* participates in S.S.R.

CUE USE

SEMANTIC

* predicts likely outcome
* uses picture cues
* substitutions retain meaning of story

SYNTACTIC

* aware of book language
* predict grammatically appropriate words and phrases.

GRAPHONIC/VISUAL

* makes predictable associations between letters and sounds
* sight vocab
* attends to punctuation

POSITIONAL/DIRECTIONAL

* processes print in left to right order
* one for one match

STRATEGIES

* self corrects
* repeats
* voice - finger point
* pause/hesitate

RESPONSE TO READING

* comments on plot
* identifies central problem
* recalls sequences of events
* re-tells the story
* identifies main characters
* comments on character traits
* infers from story

26/8
- retold the story well
- identified structure – repetitive
- trouble with 's' in 'its'
- read confidently and accurately
- said the book was "Great."
I Can Do It.
- re-reads to discover the word.
- needs to use picture cues.
- trouble with first words on a page
- "   "   ing endings.
- predicted the story line.

29/8 - Met with father & explained programme.

2/9 It Didn't Frighten Me
- retold story
- identified main character
- had trouble beginning until he remembered.
- reads 'a' for 'an'.
- using pictures when unsure of colour word - checking
- made sensible substitutions
- reading very confidently & used expression !!
- stopped when it didn't make sense.
Clever Mr. Brown.
- discussed pictures, predicting story line before reading. Responded by laughing
- began confidently
- troubled by some of the sentences
- read together

9/9 Clever Mr. Brown
Retelling: retold with all main details. Most detail about first part of story.
Identified character as ~~mean~~ not clever
Everyone knows about cars
Began wrongly but s.c. immediately
Some of terminology unfamiliar
- gas, front, rear-wheel etc.
Added 's' to words unnecessarily
- didn't pick it up
Helping
Read well
Leaving 's' off words

Written comments by the teacher on the right hand side of the page provide her with a comprehensive overview of the student's progress in reading. The checklist specifically lists the Attitudes, Strategies and Aspects of comprehension which the teacher considers appropriate for her students. Another example of a teacher reminder list is given in Appendix 14(b).

6 COMMUNICATING INFORMATION

Students, parents and caregivers need to be informed about what you define as success in your literacy program and what your general expectations of students are. For example do you expect students to:
- work independently?
- ask for help when they need it?
- take risks in their reading and writing?
- read and write a wide range of forms of writing?
- read and write for varied purposes?
- write neatly and spell correctly?
- maintain and develop their home language?

Students, parents and caregivers also need to be given feedback on how individual students are succeeding in meeting the expectations of your literacy program.

Throughout the year and at the end of the year, there may be others who need information about the student's literacy development, for example, support teachers or next year's teacher.

This chapter explores ways of:
- communicating with students, parents and caregivers about your expectations
- communicating with students, parents and caregivers about students' progress
- communicating with others.

COMMUNICATING ABOUT YOUR EXPECTATIONS
Ways of communicating with students about your expectations

Talk with students
- Explain your beliefs about learning and reasons for valuing particular ways of operating.
- Use class meetings and small group discussions to negotiate the rules, routines and expectations that will underlie the learning program.
- Use individual conferences to clarify expectations, set goals and reflect on achievements, that is to establish what needs to be done to be successful as readers and writers.

Show students what to do	• Demonstrate reading and writing strategies.
	• Show students procedures for self assessment such as:
	    how to keep records of their reading and writing experiences
	    how to analyse their own writing
	    how to review reading and writing
	    how to set realistic goals.
	• Provide a range of models in reading and writing.
	• Demonstrate how students can give feedback to each other.

Provide written guidelines for students

• Display sets of guidelines, reminder checklists and focus questions on wall charts, in "big books," or by giving students copies to paste in their own books or folders. For example one teacher has a "big book" called a *Useful Book* in which she displays sets of guidelines for reading and writing tasks. This is a set of reminders her year 2/3 students devised for finding something to write about.

Our Ideas

Look in a book.	*Write a title first.*
Look at titles.	*Make a plan.*
Look at headings.	*Use words and pictures ideas.*
Look around the room.	*Think about what you have*
Think of something special	*made.*
you have done.	*Talk to a friend.*
Look at a picture.	*Look at a topics list.*

(See Appendix 15 for a list of publishing ideas devised by year 6 students.)

Organise students' self-assessment

• Provide formats for students to set their own goals, keep records of their reading and writing, reflect on their reading and writing and identify achievements. For example one teacher uses the format below for students to set goals for their writing.

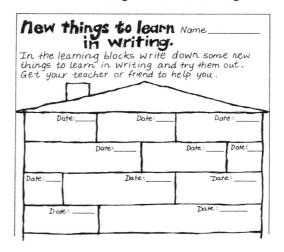

- Organise regular times for self-assessment to occur. The following is an example of a review sheet one teacher organises with his class.

NAME:

WEEK ENDING FRIDAY

This week I enjoyed...

I especially worked hard to improve...

In maths I learn about . . .

Next week in maths I would like . . .

Student comment:_____
_____
_____
_____

Teacher comment:_____
_____
_____

Parent comment:_____
_____
_____
_____

My spelling list was:

For my test I achieved   /10

This week I read...

The most interesting part I read was...

Next week I am going to read...

This week I wrote about . .

A part of my writing is below:

Next week in writing I am going to ...

Ways of communicating with parents and caregivers about your expectations

Talk with parents and caregivers

- Explain aspects of your program when talking informally to parents and caregivers e.g. before or after school, at sporting or social events, while talking on the phone.
- Encourage groups of parents and caregivers to meet to consider aspects of literacy and their children's progress.
- Where appropriate, you may seek support from the Aboriginal Education Team to assist with strategies for parent participation.

- Give information about the context in which learning occurs when talking to parents and caregivers in interviews.
- Invite parents and caregivers to information evenings at which you explain aspects of your teaching and answer questions. One teacher sends this letter of invitation to parents and caregivers early in the year.

Dear Parents,

Thank you for your response to the first note home. Your information and knowledge about your child has been invaluable for my planning and really does reinforce the important role parents play in their child's education.

A Parent Information Night will be held on_____ at_____
and will be followed by a family barbecue/get together at approximately _____
Please bring everything you need for the barbecue, meat, salads, drinks etc – the school barbecue will be available for cooking.
During the Parent Information session, details and plans for your child's education will be presented to you. Some of the areas parents have requested information on, are:

_____

_____

_____

An area which I will be speaking about will be the support parents can provide in the classroom. Parents can be involved in a number of ways as part of the reading and writing processes by listening to and reading stories with children, being an audience, discussing children's writing with them and by being another resource person.
I extend an invitation to parents to be involved in the classroom.
I anticipate the information session will last approximately one and a half hours. During the session sports equipment will be available for children to use.

If for some reason you are unable to attend the Parent Information Night and you have some concerns, please come and see me.
Hope to see you on the _____

Thanks,

- Hold workshops about exciting aspects of your program, especially those in which you hope parents and caregivers will participate. For example, teachers at one school hold workshops for the parents of Reception students which focus on strategies for supporting beginning readers.
- Arrange home visits to meet with parents and caregivers and discuss aspects of your approach.

Show parents and caregivers what students are doing

- Arrange times when parents and caregivers can visit the room to see reading and writing in action.
- Invite parents and caregivers to help in reading and writing sessions.
- Organise for students regularly to take home samples of work such as writing products, reading outcomes, self-evaluations, audio and video tapes. (See description of Communication Folder in chapter 5, on "Storing information", pp. 83-88.)
- Provide students with time and guidelines for writing to parents and caregivers about what they have been doing. This can be in the form of a personal letter, or a cooperative effort to produce a class newsletter summarising important events. (See example in Appendix 16.)

Write to parents and caregivers

- Send home a statement about your philosophy and program early in the year.
- Report on classroom activities through regular newsletters. These can take the form of a letter or you can design a quick and simple caption format.

- Send parents and caregivers written guidelines explaining particular aspects of your program and how they can support their child. Shown below are the guidelines one teacher has incorporated in the student's record sheet for reading done at home.

Reading Record

Please remember we are
LEARNERS,

so ....
- be patient when we make mistakes — we will learn from them
- enjoy reading with us .
- tell us how clever we are!
- read to us sometimes .
- talk about stories with us as we read them . eg. ask "What might happen next?"
- When we're stuck on a word help us to have a try by using all the clues on the page eg. pictures asking "What would make sense?" rereading the sentence, reading the sentence to us .

*Please remember — to contact me anytime you have any queries . — use this booklet to write any notes, comments etc.

* We learn to read by reading.

Please record the name of the book and the date read

_____
_____
_____
_____
_____
_____
_____
_____
_____
_____
_____
_____
_____
_____
_____
_____
_____
_____
_____
_____
_____
_____
_____
_____

Sometimes guidelines can be written by the students as reminders for themselves, but also serve to inform parents and caregivers about the particular activity. The following is a student's reminders for one section of her record book.

> In this part of my book I
> will respond to such things
> as:
> - Reports on group activities
> - Responses given to me by
> friends who have conferenced
> my reading/writing.
> -Opinions about my work received
> from a group of my friends/
> classmates.

• Write notes in a student's diary or a personal letter when you wish to inform parents and caregivers about an aspect of a particular student's learning program.

COMMUNICATING ABOUT STUDENTS' PROGRESS

Ways of communicating with students about their progress

Talk to students

• Use individual reading and writing conferences to discuss with students their achievements and needs.
• Use group conferences to give students immediate feedback about their writing products and reading outcomes and about the way they work in the group. Peers can also provide feedback to each other in these conferences.
• Give students immediate response as they are engaged in reading and writing tasks, e.g. "Well done Jane, you've worked out how to do that experiment by reading the instructions carefully."
• Acknowledge students' individual contributions in whole class discussions or sharing e.g. "That was an excellent summary of the first chapter Tom."

Write to students

• Record the main points of conferences for students, or help them to make a summary of these points. Students can also give each other written feedback after peer conferences. One teacher has her students fill in the form below after a peer writing conference.

Peer Conference sheet.

CONFERENCE SHEET

Date 10·11·88

Author   Title **The day I fell out of the ship**

I liked The part when you fell out of the ship.
and when you met pussy.

I wondered Why your mum said you can go on a
holiday without asking any questions.

May I suggest that you have your mum asking you
questions about the trip.

Signed

- Give students any observation notes you make that would provide useful feedback to them about their development. This can be done by giving them copies if notes are made in a carbon copy duplicating book, or you can give them the original notes to keep in their record books or folders. e.g. "17/6 Congratulations Jeff! Your 'm's' don't look like seagulls anymore!"
- Provide written feedback about their writing products or reading outcomes based on your analysis of these (or give them a copy of the analysis sheet.)
- Write replies to students' journal entries or review letters commenting on their self-evaluations and also how you view their achievements.

Celebrate students' success
- Acknowledge students' successful completion of tasks by providing opportunities for them to share them with a wider audience through displays, performances, books or newsletters.
- Organise for the audience to make a response to the work through verbal or written feedback.

Ways of communicating with parents and caregivers about students' progress

Talk to parents and caregivers
- Comment on a student's development in informal conversations with parents if it seems appropriate.

- Describe students' progress in formal interviews held at your own or the parents' request. You can illustrate your statements by showing examples from your own and students' records and also from their work.

Show parents and caregivers what students are doing

- Organise for students regularly to take home samples of work with accompanying written feedback. One teacher sends home work in a "Communication Folder" accompanied by the letter shown below.
- Send home students' self assessments and encourage parents and caregivers to discuss and respond to these.
- Set up displays, performances and other ways of sharing students' successes with parents and caregivers.

```
Dear _____

            Twice a term (Week 5 and week 10),this
folder will be sent home for you to read,comment on and
return.
    I hope it will be a way of supplying you with on-going
information about your child's progress at school.
    It will include the following:
    - A letter from your child to you or a copy of our class
newsletter.
    - A recent sample of a piece of writing.(Draft and finished
copy).
    - A review by your child on that piece of writing and on
a recently read book.
    - A copy of your child's Writing Record Chart and Reading
Record Chart.These contain a list of books read and stories
written so far this term.

    Please discuss the contents of this folder with your child.

    Could you also fill in the attached slip and return it to
school with the folder.
                                        Regards


                                        Class teacher
```

```
We have received the Parent Communication Folder dated


Together we discussed




We were most interested in




Any other comments.



                    signed
```

Write to parents and caregivers

- Inform parents and caregivers of notable achievements or concerns via diary notes or personal letters. These can be translated into the parents' home language where necessary. This feedback may also come from other people in the students' school life. For instance, at one school the principal asks teachers to report students' achievements to him, especially those of students experiencing difficulty, so that he can write a letter telling parents about their successes. This has the effect of increasing some parents' willingness to come to the school to discuss their child.
- Write formal reports that summarise aspects of the students' development. The format for these is usually negotiated by the school community, and the amount of detail necessary depends on how much communication there is through methods such as the ones already described. Two of the examples included in Appendix 17 provide room for teachers to make detailed descriptive comments, and one has a place for the student to comment. Alternatively, a separate report written entirely by the student can be sent with the teacher's report.

Dear Parents,
Below, are comments by the children regarding their own performance this year, through their own eyes. This self evaluation is not easy, yet it provides much useful information, allows children to review their work and indeed, encourages them to share in the responsibility of their learning. I would appreciate hearing any comments from you about this idea. Many thanks.

My handwriting is......
Good. Small. I am good at Storys.

In class, I am...
I am nice. I Share With my friends I Sit Still.

• My Progress Information Sheet •

Name :

Class : A
Year Level : 1988 Year 2
Age : 8

I think my writing is .... (why?)
I help myself with my work. I have a try at my words, I re-read my stories and correct them.

I think my reading is .... (why?)
I read lots of hard Books. Duggy Dogs Books are my favourite

I think my maths is .... (why?)
I think my Maths is excellent. I do lots of Sums. I have learnt to Measure.

My favourite thing at school is..... plays computers

I think I'm best at.... Sharing

signed :

(Additional examples are shown in Appendix 17.)

COMMUNICATING WITH OTHERS

There will be occasions when you need to communicate about your expectations and students' progress to other people who are involved in their learning program. During the school year these may include:

- support personnel from outside the school e.g. guidance officers or special education teachers
- support personnel within the school e.g. specialist teachers, ESL teachers, Aboriginal Education Workers, bi-lingual aides
- teachers in other schools, in the case of students transferring.

At the end of the school year you will make decisions about what you need to communicate to your students' next teachers. These decisions may be governed by school policy or by what the next teacher considers most useful.

The ways you communicate with these people will be the same as those used with parents, but your focus will vary depending on what information is specifically required.

Talk with others

- Discuss aspects of your program and the student's development in interviews or on the phone. You may want to write a supporting summary to hand on as well.

Show others what the student is doing

- Use your own and the student's records and samples of the student's work, to illustrate the points you make in interviews.
- Pass on the student's record folder and record book to the student's new teacher (either during the year or at the end of the year.) If a student is starting at a new school during the year, the student will also have the work already done in your class to show. When a student is moving to another teacher at the end of the year, only selected samples will be passed on, possibly accompanied by the reasons for choosing them and any written analyses. For NESB students, some or all, of these samples may be in their home language.
- Consider the value of giving the student's next teacher copies of formal reports you have written about the student. Some schools have a policy of passing these on from year to year.

Write to others

- Fill in specific details on set formats where this is required by the individual or group requesting the information (e.g. Special Education Units or Guidance and Special Services.) Some teachers design their own format for summarising information about students' development or their teaching program. The example below is designed by one teacher to communicate some main points about the student's learning experiences to the student's next teacher.

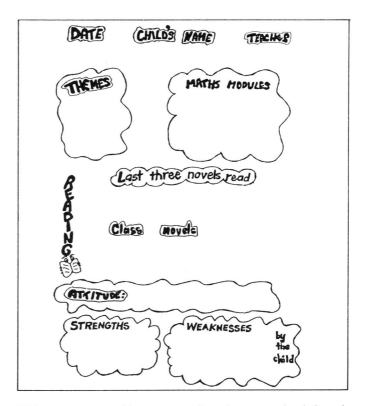

- Write a summary of important points about a student's learning experiences and progress to send on when a student transfers, or to give information to support personnel.
- Write a summary of the main features of your program to give to the student's next teacher at the end of the year. It will be a general overview of what the student has participated in and your particular areas of focus.

APPENDICES

THE CAASR FRAMEWORK

CONCEPTS ABOUT LITERACY

ATTITUDES TO WRITING	ATTITUDES TO READING

ASPECTS OF WRITTEN PRODUCTS	ASPECTS OF READING COMPREHENSION

STRATEGIES FOR WRITING	STRATEGIES FOR READING

RANGE OF WRITING AND READING FORMS AND PURPOSES

APPENDIX 2: ASSESSMENT PLAN: WRITING - One teacher's overview chart

What	How	Who does it	When	Documentation	Program Implications/Action
Concepts/ Attitudes, Writing	• Survey sheet, expectations strengths/weaknesses (Parents)	Parents	T1, Wk1, new entrants	Survey sheet (Parent)	• Organise Parent meetings re class reading/writing programme. Establish borrowing routines, procedures for learning program, "Home reading."
	• Survey sheet, interests, strengths/weaknesses (Students)	Student	T1, Wk1, new entrants	Survey sheet (Student)	• Set up information/display board for parents, brochures and parent booklets available.
	• Student written progress reports	Student	End of each term	Proforma, "Things I can do in writing," "New things to learn." To go home with progress reports	• Set up routine for writing sessions : use of personal dictionaries, word charts/writing resources, conferencing procedure etc.
	• Observations	Teacher	Ongoing	Observations notebook/desk chart	• Establish writing/reading activity sessions and set purpose for these.
	• Reviews' student written	Student	Twice a term	Review Sheet	• Begin L.C.W.C. procedure for spelling and establish
	• Informal parent contact	Teacher/Parent	Ongoing	Notebook	as a learning process.
Strategies in Pre-writing	• Personal Topic Lists	Student	Ongoing, review reg.	Topic list proforma in books	• Compile charts, guidelines, focus questions for 3
	• Pre-writing discussion	Teacher/student small group	Ongoing	Focus chart, guided questions	stages of writing process, encourage independent use.
	• Observation	Teacher	Ongoing	Notebook jottings/desk chart	• Demonstrating/modelling procedures/strategies for
	• Modelled writing sessions	Student/Teacher	Ongoing	Writing charts, "Before Writing" sheet.	use.
Writing	• What can I do in writing?	Student/Teacher Teacher/	Ongoing writing times Mid T1, mid T3	"Achievements" balloons form	• Class brainstorming of possible writing ideas,chart.
	• Spelling features analysis	Student, special needs		Analysis sheet	• Decide with class selection procedures for publishing.
	• Samples of product	Teacher	2 per term	Photocopy of product, analysis form	• Organise workshop/s for parent volunteers in supporting reading/writing in class.
	• L.C.W.C. procedure, spelling	Student/Teacher	Ongoing	"Spelling" books for child practise.	• Covering letter/s with stuff sent home viz survey.
Post-Writing	• Writing I have done/published	Student	Ongoing	Proforma in writing journals	
	• Editing guidelines	Student/Teacher conferences	Ongoing	Focus chart with guidelines	
	• Writing we have Published," shelf in class library	Student	Ongoing	Chart, "Writing we have Published."	
Aspects of written products	• Product sample (Teacher selected)	Teacher	6 times a year	Product analysis framework Student written "Progress" report in writing. Store in "Student Learning File."	
	• Product sample (Student selected)	Teacher			

APPENDIX 2 (continued): ASSESSMENT PLAN: READING - One teacher's overview chart

What	How	Who does it	When	Documentation	Program Implications/Action
Concepts/ Attitudes, Reading	• Personal Reading Record. • School Library borrowing trends. • Parent survey. • 'Concepts about Print' - M. Clay. • Observations in 'Reading Activities.'	Student/Teacher/ Parent Teacher/Librarian/ Student Parents Teacher/Students with special needs Teacher	Ongoing. Ongoing. T1, with writing survey. Early T1, new entrants, review T3. Ongoing, during sessions.	"Books I have borrowed" card in "Take Home bag." Record independent or required support. Returned survey proforma. Record sheets in guide book. Observations notebook/desk chart.	• Explain with Librarian functional record card and procedure for filing it out. • Oranise with Librarian functional class file for borrowing trends. • Provision in play activity times for roving and observing reading/writing behaviour where self-selected. • Set up "Books I have at home" area for display.
Strategies - Natural/Basic	• Oral reading performance. • Observations in reading task. • Cloze procedures. • Guided reading sessions. • Observation of 'silent reading behaviour.'	Teacher/Student, 1-1 Teacher Student/Teacher (groups) Student/Teacher (groups) Teacher	2 'formal' times per term - Ongoing. Ongoing, class activites. Ongoing, class activities. Ongoing.	Anecdotal records in notebook. Notebook jottings/desk chart. Cloze sheets, published and teacher made; teacher jottings on sheets. Program notes, notebook jottings. Notebook jottings/desk chart.	• Allow for recording in notebook observations during/after sessions. • Set up structures/procedures for guided reading sessions. etc., work out grouping patterns for teaching/learning, parent support. • Expectations for those not involved in 'Teacher-time,' independent activites.
Coping Strategies	• Running Records. • Observation. • Guided reading sessions.	Teacher/Students with special needs Special Education teacher (Students with special needs.)	Once a term. When required.	Recording process in guidebook/proformas. Records kept by Special Education teacher.	• Selection of any published material to be used - cloze passages, O.H. transparencies, passages for retelling procedure, charts and reading material to be used.
Aspects of Comprehension • **Inclusive of fiction and non-fiction texts**	• Retelling tasks (oral and written). • Responses to Literature in Art, Drama, Play etc. • Guided reading sessions. • 'Question the Text' procedure. • Sequencing tasks (organisation of texts). • 'Purposes for reading,' charted. Record range of literary format. • 'Book Talk sessions.' • Story mapping procedure. • Book 'Reviews'.	Teacher/Student group or 1-1 Student Student/Teacher group or 1-1 Student, group or 1-1 Student, group or 1-1 Teacher, class group Student/Teacher, 'circle format.' Student, individual/ group Student	Ongoing, class program. Ongoing, class program. Ongoing, teaching program. Ongoing, class program. Ongoing, class program. Review termly. Weekly, class program. Ongoing, class program. Ongoing, class program.	Format suggested in handbook, record sheets provided. Program notes, displays, kids books, class books etc. Notebook jottings, 'follow-up' activities/desk chart. "Questions" charts. Task cards, notebook jottings/ desk chart. Class charts, colour code after exposure' to form/genre. "Book Reviews" proforma or record oral reviews in notebook/desk chart. Program, students' product'. Review proformas.	• Program to include daily independent reading sessions, daily writing, L.C.W.C. practice regularly, "Book Talk" sessions, modelled writing. • Teacher's aide support in running off proformas, sheets, etc. so a stock of them available. • Decide on record keeping, where information stored and what needs to be kept. • Consider 'new entrants' as year progresses, what information needed when entered. • Implement 'peer-tutoring' system to allow for support systems in reading/writing. • Teaching selecting strategies for book borrowing.

APPENDIX 3: YEARLY ASSESSMENT DIARY: one example

	TERM 1	TERM 2	TERM 3	TERM 4
1	Check previous records in 'Student Learning Files'/where possible/necessary talk with previous teacher/informal contact with parents. Distribute Parent survey. Begin desk 'Observations sheet.' Pre-writing discussion for student survey or 'Me as a Writer.'	Review, extend 'Ideas for Writing' proforma, 'Writing to Try.'	Review, extend 'Ideas for Writing' proforma, 'Writing to Try.'	Review, extend 'Ideas for Writing' proforma, 'Writing to Try.'
2	Pre-writing discussion re student survey on reading, later in week student complete. Introduce proforma 'Writing Ideas and Writing to Try' and do a group modelling lesson.' Begin 'Reading/Writing' activities sessions for informal observation purposes.	Review L.C.W.C. procedure if suiting needs of students. Changes in writing vocabulary.	Look at writing vocab. task from T1 and expand new vocabulary.	
3	Introduce proforma 'Things I can do in writing,' discuss purpose and sorts of indicators for inclusion. Needs of E.S.L. learners with E.S.L. teacher. Distribute 'Writing I have done/Published' proforma. Explain students look back over writing and record needed information.	ONGOING 'Things I can do in writing' 'New things to learn in writing' 'Writing I have done' proforma, continue Reading/Writing activities sessions for informal observations	Review Special Edn. support groups needs for further development.	ONGOING Things I can do in Writing, 'New things to learn in Writing,' 'Writing I have done' proforma, continue Reading/Writing sessions for informal observations.
4	Parent meeting, 'Program Review.' (Go over proposed learning program, teaching style etc., concerns Parents may have. Suggestions for home help in brochure.) 'Write all the words you know how to spell' task. Introduce L.C.W.C. procedure.		ONGOING 'Things I can do in writing,' 'New things to learn in Writing,' 'Writing I have done' proforma, continue Reading/Writing activities sessions for informal observations.	
5	Introduce focus charts for writing process, explain purpose/use etc. Initiate 'Special Edn.' support for any students at risk (further assessment if needed."			Begin oral reading performance analysis and running records where needed.
6	'Concepts About Print' test - M. Clay, students with special needs. 'Oral Reading Performance' analysis. 'Running Records' for students with special needs.	'Oral Reading Performance' analysis. 'Running Records' for students with special needs. Review needs, further development of E.S.L. group.	Begin product analysis in writing from collected samples. 'Concepts About Print' test, M. Clay student special needs. Oral reading performance analysis. Running Records for students with special needs.	Begin product analysis in writing from collected samples. Review Personal Reading records for range of texts read, growth in complexity etc.
7	Students writing own 'Progress Reports' in preparation for interviews Wk 8. Discuss format etc, collect product examples for Parents to see. 'Spelling Features' analysis (Students with special needs.) Review Personal Reading Records for range/text type/indep. or support reading.	Students writing own 'Progress Reports' in preparation for interviews Wk 8. Discuss format etc. beforehand. Collect product examples for parents to see. Review Personal Reading Records for range, text type, if independent or 'read-along.'	Student writing own 'Progress Reports' for interviews Wk 8, collect samples of work etc. 'Spelling features analysis' (Students with special needs.) Review Personal reading records.	Student writing final 'Progress Report' for interviews Wk 8, collect samples of work etc. Continue product analysis in writing from collected samples. Distribute Parent Evaluation sheets for discussion in Wk 8.
8	Check borrowing trends from school library file. Skim notebook jottings for information. Parent interviews (oral only.) Distribute evaluation/review sheet.	Check borrowing trends from School Library. Skim notebook jottings for information. Parent interviews (written report.) Distribute evaluation/review sheet.	Check borrowing trends from School Library. Skim notebook jottings for information. Parent interviews (oral only.) Distribute evaluation/review sheet.	Check borrowing trends from School Library. Skim notebook jottings for information. Parent interviews (written report.) Distribute evaluation/review sheet.
9	Product analysis from collected samples of writing		Review E.S.O. groups needs with T.E.S.L. teacher for T4. Look at L.C.W.C. procedure for continued growth, introduce Try Basic word List if needed by individuals for T4.	Collecting product samples, reading records, writing development proformas etc. for placement in 'student Learning File.' Program evaluation.
10/11	Program evaluation.	Program evaluation.	Program evaluation.	Filing in 'Student Learning Profiles.'
	Filing in 'Student Learning Profiles.'	Filing in 'Student Learning Profiles.'	Filing in 'Student Learning Profiles.'	

APPENDIX 4: WEEKLY ASSESSMENT TIMETABLE: one example

WEEKLY TIMETABLE SHOWING SOME TYPICAL LITERACY ASSESSMENT OPPORTUNITIES

	Monday	Tuesday	Wednesday	Thursday	Friday
9.00					
9.20	**Writing** *Individual teacher/student conferences and peer conferences*				**Directed Language Arts Activities** *Teacher can review individual students' progress.*
10.00	*Teacher can observe and record aspects of writing whilst students write*				
10.20	**Group conference** *Teacher can observe and record whilst students conduct group conferences, whole class or small groups*				
10.40	RECESS				
10.55			**Library** *Teacher can observe and record reading habits, attitudes etc*		
11.30					
12.30	LUNCH				
1.25	**Reading** *Teacher/student reading conferences can be held for part of this reading period*				
2.00	**Directed Language Arts Activities** *Time for 'catch-up' conferences if necessary*		**Directed Language Arts Activities** *Time for 'catch-up' conferences if necessary*		**Weekly Review** *Students' written self-assessments.*
2.30	**Teacher non-instructional time** *Parent interviews if necessary*		**Teacher non-instructional time** *Analysis of students' written products*		

Teacher's weekend task: Read and respond to student self-assessments

Writing Analysis Sheet

Name: _____

Title/Topic: _____

Date: _____

Language: _____

Ideas	Language
Organisation	Mechanics

Child's writing:

I AM HPIE
BCOS
I HA
BN TO VIDHB!!
♥ MUM ♥

Child read as:

I am happy
because
I have
been to Victor Harbor
I love
Mummy

Writing Analysis Sheet

Name: Tanya

Title (Topic): About her trip to Victor Harbor

Date: 11/11/88

Free choice. After a visit to Victor Harbor by family

Ideas
- written for self
- related to own experience
- presents 2 ideas
- elaborates on why she's happy (because)

Language
- simple words
- writes as she talks
- compound sentence linked with because

Organisation
- description of feelings
- statement – I am happy
- reasons – I have been to Victor Harbor

Mechanics
- left to right, down page
- spaces
- letters / capitals
- spelling (am, to) using end of words (mummy)
- uses sound / symbol connections bcos (because) VIDHB (Victor Harbor)

108

The Ghost and the child 9/2/88
One dark night I decided to go for a walk. I walked past the cemetery and a ghost popped out. The ghost said to me, "do you want to come down to the my coffin" - I said "yes". I went down and I said to the ghost "will is like a little room". The ghost said to me I want to tell you a ghost story. The story began when he said "One spooky night a witch set a spell on a little girl. The spell was that she grew and father and father POP! she went all over the floor into one hundred pieces. I said to the ghost "I've got to go home now but I will come back tomorrow" I went home and fell straight to sleep. In the morning I told my mother and father about it. But they did not believe me. I ran down to my bedroom and I saw the ghost at my window I opened the window - and the ghost came in father showed my mother and father that the ghost could keep him. The family and the ghost lived happily ever after.

Writing Analysis Sheet

Name: Zara
Title/Topic: The Ghost + the child
Date: 9.2.88
Free Choice Topic: At start of school year

Ideas
- writing for others
- conventional view of ghosts, witches.
- ideas are fantasy based

Organisation
- Story form - setting (where, who, when)
  problem (about sth)
  episodes
  resolution
  outcome
- focus - title suits story
  - introduction sets scene
- puts a small story in a story.

Language
- consistency of fantasy language; Once upon a time, Happily ever after.
- range of words appropriate to story; cemetery, ghost, coffin, dark night etc
- varied sentence beginnings and length
- use of dialogue

Mechanics
- even handwriting
- letters well formed, evenly spaced
- spelling - correct spelling
  - self corrected
- punctuation - stops, capitals commas, speech, exclamation apostrophic
- uses enlarged print and capitals for emphasis - POP!

To FATORISMAS
I AM LOC/FOWAD
aTILCRISMAS.
I LOVE YOU.
YOU UR PRITIYASA9!
OEUVP BOO
CANIPLISE
haFo ASK ME
Dosee LOVE FBOM NIKKI

And read:
To Father Christmas,
I am looking forward
until Christmas.
I love you.
You are pretty as
a coloured bird.
Can I please
have a Ask he
Dabar.   Love from

Writing Analysis Sheet

Name: Nikki

Title/Topic: Christmas letter

Date: 12/11/88

Written after discussion on Father Christmas. Free choice

Ideas	Language
· understands that readers like nice things said about them - stated this way. (met needs of others)	· range appropriate · uses simile "You are as pretty as a coloured bird" · varied sentence beginnings · appropriate tone.

Organisation	Mechanics

· organised in letter format (, love from)
· maintained focus of a letter
· 3 separate parts.
	· left to right, down page
	· uses invented spelling
	  - culd (coloured)
	  - haf (have)
	  - fowad (forward)
	· spaces between words
	· uses sound/symbol relationships
	· uses full stops, capitals
	· upper/lower case letters
	· picture illustrates story

APPENDIX 6: READING – EXAMPLES OF FOCUS QUESTIONS

Setting

1. What is the setting for the story? (where?)
2. Are there different settings within the story? What are they? Why are there different settings?
3. What time was it set in? How do you know?
4. Does the story move about in time? (Could it be shown by a time line?)
5. What effect does the setting have on the character?
   .... on the plot?
6. Select sections that clearly describe the setting.
7. Could you identify with that type of setting?
8. Draw/map/illustrate/make models of the setting.
9. Did the setting become clearer as the story moved on?
10. How realistic is the setting?

Plot

1. What was the major happening in the story?
2. What was the sequence of events?
3. How was the problem resolved? Were you happy with this way?
4. Which characters were mainly involved in the conflict?
5. Give another resolution/ending to the problem/story.
6. Could there be a sequel to this story? What?
7. Could the story really have happened?
8. Did it - or parts - surprise you in any way? How?
9. Have you read similar stories? Which? In what ways?
10. How might the story change if set in a different time?

    different place?

    different characters?

Theme

1. Can you identify a particular theme in the story?
2. What sorts of feelings are aroused in you?
3. Are there certain aspects of life you can better understand now? e.g. loneliness/ growing up/death ....
4. Were there definite ideas of what is good and what is bad?

Style

1. How did the author, through language, create moods?
2. Was the style easy for you to read? Why?
3. Were there changes in style/pace to keep your interest up?
4. Were there pieces/sections that you didn't like?
5. Can you think of other books that were similar in style? Which? How?

WRITER'S CHECKLIST
QUESTIONS WRITER'S SHOULD ASK THEMSELVES AFTER THE FIRST DRAFT.

MY IDEAS
Does the title reflect the main ideas?
Did I talk to others about my ideas before writing?
Have I expressed my own thoughts, feelings or opinions?
Have I clearly presented and developed the main ideas?

MY ORGANISATION
Does my beginning create interest?
Have I structured my writing to include — a setting
Have I used sub-headings or paragraphs? — a problem (mystery)
Are the links between events clear? — episodes (chapters)
Is my ending satisfying? — outcome (of problem)
— conclusion (ending)

LANGUAGE
Does the length of the sentences vary to assist the flow?
Have I used varied and interesting sentence beginnings?
Have I used interesting and precise words?
Have I checked to avoid repetitive words?
Does the language suit the intended audience?
Do my paragraphs help build atmosphere?
Have I read it aloud to see how it sounds?
Has anyone else read it and discussed it with me?

MECHANICS
Have I used the editing checklist for correct punctuation?
Have I circled possible spelling errors?
Have I used other sources to check these words?
Have I checked the general layout?
Can others read my writing with ease?

↓

2nd, 3rd or 4th draft ?!!
..... and then a teacher conference

APPENDIX 8a: WRITING RECORD SHEET - Example 1

WRITING RECORD   NAME _____

Date			
Title			
Purpose for writing			
Achievements			
Challenges/ In progress			
Teaching points Reminder			

APPENDIX 8b: WRITING RECORD SHEET- Example 2

WRITING RECORDS

NAME:

CAAS	TITLE ___ DATE ___ FOCUS ___	TITLE ___ DATE ___ FOCUS ___	TITLE ___ DATE ___ FOCUS ___	TITLE ___ DATE ___ FOCUS ___	TITLE ___ DATE ___ FOCUS ___
Concepts of Literacy					
Attitudes - Self-Concept - Commitment					
Aspects of Written Products - Ideas - Organisation - Language - Mechanics					
Strategies - Pre-Writing - Writing - Post-Writing					

Writing Record

Child's Name	
Attitudes	**Observations**
	(dated anecdotal notes)
Process	
1. Pre-writing	
2. Writing	
3. Post writing	

Strengths		Challenges	
Date		Date	

NOVEL NAG NOTES

TITLE: _____

AUTHOR: _____

MAIN CHARACTERS: _____

RATING: _____

***** EXCELLENT   ** FAIR
**** VERY GOOD   * BORING
***   GOOD

SETTING: (where the story took place) _____

PLOT: (what happened) _____

_____

COMMENT: (your opinion) _____

_____

PAGE TO READ ALOUD: _____

TEACHER COMMENT: _____

DATE: _____

APPENDIX 10: READING RECORD SHEET

READING RECORD   NAME _____

FOCUS for weeks _____ to _____			
Type of activity			
	Title _____ Date _____	Title _____ Date _____	Title _____ Date _____
Achievements			
Challenges/ Progress			
Teaching Points Reminders			

APPENDIX 11a: READING REFERENCE SHEET

Reading Behaviours/Strategies
- performs fluently from favourite books
- uses sentence patterns
- distinguishes between print/picture
- uses pictures cues
- scans from left to right
- goes from top to bottom of page
- uses word by word match
- uses initial letters
- uses final letters
- recognises sight words (a,the,etc)
- attends to punctuation
- finger points
- re-reads
- repeats words or phrases
- "voice" points
- stops when not making sense
- predicts using - semantic
    syntactic
    knowledge of the world.

Concepts about Literacy
- uses for reading
- kinds of texts -   fiction
                    non-fiction
- differences between speech & writing
- reading processes.

Attitudes
- chooses to read
- borrows books regularly/ frequently
- reads wide variety of books
- self selects appropriately
- shares with others
- reads for sustained periods of time.

Influences:
- expectations based on racial or gender stereo typing
- sexual, racial or other forms of harassment
- attitudes to disabilities
- recency of migration and learning English
- acknowledgement and valuing of students' experiences, culture and home language
- range of books available in home language.

Responses to Reading - Fiction:
- comments on plot
- identifies central problem
- recalls sequences of events
- re-tells the story
- identifies main characters
- comments on character traits
- talks about likes and dislikes.

Responses to Reading - Non Fiction:
- skim reads
- underlines difficult words
- uses other resources
- asks questions
- makes notes, diagrams.

To place at front of Teacher's Record Folder

READING BEHAVIOURS/STRATEGIES	CONCEPTS ABOUT LITERACY
	ATTITUDES
	INFLUENCES
	RESPONSES TO READING – FICTION
	RESPONSES TO READING – NON FICTION

Observation sheet for _____

focus:

Russ	Clayton	Erin	Laura	Rohan
Tristram				
Joel	Tom	Cole	Gareth	Losni
Nicole	Amber	Barry	Brooke	Corey
Blake	Sime	Tyrone	Amy	Tania
Christopher	Emily	Justin	Ntina	Yahna

APPENDIX 11d: READING OBSERVATION RECORD

Date													
RESOURCE CENTRE													
Approp. library manners													
used catalogue													
found books efficiently													
went straight to section													
selected efficiently													
wandered about													
selected slowly													
sought assistance													
selected approp. level													
other comments													
(selection made/how....)													
SILENT READING TIME													
settled quickly													
settled in due course!													
totally absorbed													
absorbed spasmodically													
read short period													
distracted													
wanted to share													
other comments													

(Retype, selecting appropriate questions and leaving spaces between questions for students' replies.)

Interest Inventory

Name _____

Age _____

Birthday _____

This is a picture of me
or
This is my finger print

My lucky number is...

The people in my family are...

The people who live in my house are...

I help at home by...

My best friends are...

I like people who...

When I'm bored, I like to...

The sports I play or would like to play are...

My interests and hobbies are...

Clubs to belong to are...

The pets in my family are...

My favourite T.V. programs/videos are...

My favourite song is...

The best book I read last year was...

The most exciting thing I have ever done was...

I worry about..

Something I would like to change about the world is...

My favourite thing at school is...........................because ...

My least favourite thing at school is...........................because...

I would like to learn more about...

This year at school I want to improve at...

I am good at...

Me as a writer

Make this face look how
you feel as a writer

Name_____

The kinds of writing I like to do are ....

I like writing when ....

I am better at ....

I now want to get better at ....

APPENDIX 14a: REFERENCE LIST FOR CUMULATIVE RECORDS OF STUDENT WRITING PROGRESS (To be kept inside Teacher Cumulative Record Folder)

CONCEPTS
- uses for writing
- forms/genres/kinds/appropriateness
- audiences
- speech/writing relationships
- processes
- cultural - social influences.

ATTITUDES
- self-concept in writing
- time/energy commitment
- risk-taking
- responsibility
- attitude to change
- help seeking
- suspend judgement
- stay on task
- share with peers
- influences

STRATEGIES
- pre-writing strategies
- writing/revising strategies
- post-writing strategies
- use of resources.

ASPECTS OF WRITTEN PRODUCTS:

Ideas and Information
Topic knowledge
- amount of information
- depth
- accuracy
- different kinds of information
- relating information from other sources

Knowledge of the world
- understandings of themselves and others
- relationships
- community
- natural environment

Presentation of Ideas
- rationality
- explain
- elaborate
- own opinions
- different perspectives

Organisation
- form/kind/genre
- focus
- parts
- sequences
- links
- readers' needs.

Language
- vocabulary
- sentence structure
- style
- atmosphere/mood
- voice
- consistency.

Mechanics
- handwriting
- spelling
- punctuation
- layout
- word processing.

NAME

CONCEPTS	**ASPECTS OF WRITTEN PRODUCTS**
	Ideas
	Organisation
ATTITUDES	
	Language
STRATEGIES	
	Mechanics

Different Ways of
<u>PUBLISHING</u>

As a card

A Flip-book

An advertisement

On — cardboard
    cartridge
    coloured paper
    blackboard

As a book

In a book (language)

As a project

Have it typed

As a comic book — Hi!

As a diary / log / journal

As a letter - post it!   In a scrapbook

As a play, using scripts
    "   ·   ", using puppets   On tape!

As a scroll   As a pamphlet

As a menu   In a code ˑ⋏0x⊷ː

Using the computer

Act it out

As a poster
magazine
newspaper
newsletter
poetry book
cook book
song book ♫

Using photos

As a recipe - cook it!

As a report

AND MANY MORE!!

APPENDIX 16: NEWSLETTER (Excerpts only)

YEAR 5/6
◀NEWS LETTER▶

S.A.P.S.A.S.A.

This term I went to Berri for running. I came 2nd in the 200 metre and 3rd in the 100 metre race. Two weeks later I went to Adelaide for the 100 metre relay. We came 3rd in the first heat and 4th in the finals. We just missed out on a medal.

by

Olympics
Days of sweating
Sportsmanship and friendship
And then finally
Winning
Gold!

by

I
I like
I like this
I like this term
I like this term because
I like this term because we
I like this term because we went
I like this term because we went to
I like this term because we went to Burra.
I like this term because we went to Burra.

It's nearly holidays so look out Mum and Dad! It This term we made 200 bags of popcorn to raise money for the Burra camp. It was the only fund raising this we had. The rest of the money came out of the camp costs. Burra was great. We stayed at Redruth Camp Centre. It is an old church. It was huge. The thing I liked best was being guided around Burra by Mrs. Pearce. I reckon we went to every tourist attraction in Burra. I thought it was interesting to see the Burra Burra Mine and the Bon Accord Mine.

I really enjoyed Mt. Gambier because we stayed at the Pine Lodge Centre for the week. We also went to Blue Lake, ten pin bowling and the heated swimming pool. I liked the people who were at Pine Lodge because they were friendly. They also spoilt us all week. Mt. Gambier was the best trip I've ever been on with the school.

by

REPORT ON THE

ACHIEVEMENTS

OF

_____

I am good at:

....

....

....

....

GENERAL COMMENTS

TEACHER _____

PRINCIPAL _____

DATE _____

APPENDIX 17a: STUDENT/TEACHER WRITTEN REPORTS - Blank example (continued)

SOCIAL SKILLS

ASSESSMENT FOLDER

Children are born with differing abilities so we should not judge a child's progress by comparison with other children, even those in the same family. Provided children are developing according to their capacity and are happily adjusted socially, teachers and parents should not feel concerned.

GENERAL COMMENT

Teacher's Signature ——————— Date— /— /—

Principal's Signature ——————— Date— /— /—

NAME

CLASS TEACHER

DATE

Parent's Comments

Signature ——————— Date— /— /—

Child's Comments

Signature ——————— Date— /— /—

APPENDIX 17b: STUDENT/TEACHER WRITTEN REPORTS – completed example

Term 1   Student Report

Name: Date:

Comment on each of these aspects of your work

Give yourself a rating in the box for each area of work.

Red Fantastic	Green Going Well	Brown Needs more effort

Language

Books I've read

I did fairly well with my reading this term. I read a few Colin Thiele books and really enjoyed them. I tried to read every night so I could read a few books. The most interesting book would of been the hammerhead light.

Reading Diary

With my reading diary I've been trying hard to get it in on time I've been writing manly a page about the book. I've been trying to get the presentation done nicely and to correct the spelling so I dont make mistakes

Group Discussion

I think I could listen a bit more carefully to what the person is reading out I also think I should try and think of some more questions I could give to the persons

Plays

Our group co cooperate well and try to do quickly if we really have to. I think we could try and think of them before hand so we know what were doing and people can get costumes ready

Reading Activities

I liked doing my reading activities and I put a lot of work into it The best one I think would have to be my story map. I liked writing the letter to Shaun and doing the book review.

Spelling

Most of my spelling is alright I like it when we do our own words and do the activities for them.

Words I need to concentrate on are.... unconsaous and sergeant

Creative Writing

In writing I have learnt about...... how to use direct speech and how you start a new line and where to put the comma in I have also learnt about words to use instead of "said"

I need to pay attention to .... thinking of something different to start a sentence

Social Studies / Health / Science

I have learnt about....
I have where the Fleurieu Penisula is and lots of the towns that are in it In science I have how learnt how terreble it is that the whales are getting beached and how people are cutting down the animals enviroment

Music

I choir I have learnt a bit more about notes I have liked singing the songs that I already know like the three beatles songs thatt we are going to sing for choir

P.E.

In pe I would like to play more kick it crecket with Mrs Brumbaur. I have liked doing the with Mrs Brumbauer but would like to do more games outside.

German

In German I have liked doing the little plays and playing the other games that we've played I liked going in our groups and having the set of cutlery and asking for different thing

Art/Craft

I liked decorating the room with our seaweed and fish. I would like to do what the year sevens did with the nails and wood I would also like to do some crafty things with wool like knotting.

Homework I have been trying very hard to get my homework done on time and I usually read each night.

Neatness in books I have been trying very hard to get my neatness in my books and I'm happy with the writing in my reading diary

Joanne T

Comment on some of the things you have enjoyed this term.
I enjoyed doin our story maps and setting them out. I liked decorating the room to make it look like the sea. I liked doing the research for our projects and I'm looking forward to writing them out.

Next term I would like to....
try to go over more than 33 cones and do well on the 4055 country run. Also I would like to do better with my Maths and concentrate harder

Teacher comment
It's great to see some of the excellent work you can do Joanne. Keep up the good work.
Signed

Signed _____

132

Review 1

Name: _____

Month Ending: _____

This month I enjoyed most _____

I especially worked hard to improve _____

My best achievement was _____

I organise my time well

I prioritise my activities

I settle to work

I work well independently

I take care with presentation

I solve problems as they arise

I seek help when needed

I assist others when required

I take responsibility for my actions

I work co-operatively

I stay on task

I choose not to be distracted by others

I choose resources I need wisely

I look at things with an overview

I use and show self-discipline

I evaluate my behaviour realistically and honestly

(Choose from: always, often never, true, false, try, don't understand)

Teacher's comment:- _____

Signed: _____

Parent's comment: _____

Signed: _____

SOCIAL EDUCATION:

This month·I _____

I liked _____

MUSIC/ART/DRAMA:

PHYS-ED: I have been learning _____

LANGUAGE:

At present I am READING _____

I am enjoying it because _____

My favourite novel of the month was _____

because _____

This month I have enjoyed WRITING _____

I'm pleased with _____

Next month I plan to _____

I think my SPELLING is _____

Some new words I have used in my writing are _____

MATHS:

This month I have learnt _____

In MENTAL ARITHMETIC I averaged _____